D1380330

FOR BREW
FREAKS,
BEAN
GEEKS,
AND
THE
SIMPLY
CURIOUS ...

SCOTTISH
INDEPENDENT
COFFEE
GUIDE

the INSIDER'S GUIDE TO SPECIALITY
COFFEE VENUES AND ROASTERS

★ ★ ★ ★ ★ ★ ★ ★ ★ ★

№ 2

Salt Media, 5 Cross Street, Devon, EX31 1BA.
www.saltmedia.co.uk
Tel: 01271 859299 Email: ideas@saltmedia.co.uk

Salt Media *Independent Coffee Guide* team:
Nick Cooper, Lucy Deasy, Kathryn Lewis, Lisa McNeil,
Tamsin Powell, Jo Rees, Rosanna Rothery,
Emma Scott-Goldstone, Chris Sheppard, Dale Stiling,
Katie Taylor and Mark Tibbles.
Design and illustration: Salt Media

**A big thank you to the *Scottish Independent Coffee Guide*
committee** (meet them on page 150) for their expertise
and enthusiasm, **our headline sponsors** Cimbali,
KeepCup and Schluter, **and sponsors** Cakesmiths,
Dear Green Coffee Roasters, Speciality Coffee
Association and Salt Media. **Special thanks to
photographer** Gavin Smart for his work on the guide.

Coffee shops, cafes and roasters are invited to be
included in the guide based on meeting criteria set
by our committee, which includes use of speciality
beans, a high quality coffee experience and being
independently run.

All references to the Speciality Coffee Association of
Europe (SCAE) and the Speciality Coffee Association of
America (SCAA) have been changed to the Speciality
Coffee Association (SCA) to reflect the merging of the
two organisations in January 2017.

For information on the Scottish, South West and South
Wales, and Northern *Independent Coffee Guides*, visit:
www.indycoffee.guide

🐦 @indycoffeeguide 📷 @indycoffeeguide

THOMSON'S COFFEE ROASTERS
№ 101

CONTENTS

Page

WELCOME

t's remarkable to witness the explosion of Scotland's speciality coffee scene since we launched the guide a year ago.

We've seen some cool new additions pop up across the country this year, and the sheer quantity of new speciality cafes in Edinburgh is particularly astounding.

What's so thrilling for coffee lovers is the breadth of caffeinated experiences on offer – from geeky gaffs where it's all about the brew, to delectable foodie spots where the coffee is as good as the grub – and we all know that's not easy to find.

'STONKING GRILLED CHEESE TOASTIES AND KID-IN-A-SWEETIE-SHOP ROASTERIES'

BRING YOUR OWN Cup.

We've added a new symbol to the cafes this year, identifying places where you can take your own reusable cup. Read more about how the speciality coffee industry is embracing sustainability on page 20.

This year our explorations have unearthed community enterprises, healthy eating coffee haunts, sharp-edged modernism and nostalgic elegance, as well as stonking grilled cheese toasties and kid-in-a-sweetie-shop roasteries – and it's all here for you to get stuck into.

So take yourself on a coffee tour and slurp down some new finds and old faves. All the businesses included are independent, provide a top-notch speciality coffee experience and importantly, are doing it with love.

Enjoy!

Jo Rees
Editor
Indy Coffee Guides

🐦 @indycoffeeguide
📷 @indycoffeeguide

BEAN SCENE

From espresso fuelled basement gigs to latte art smackdowns in the back room and off-the-cuff cupping sessions, Scotland's thriving underground speciality scene is gaining serious momentum

Forget cafe doors closing at four and a ticking off for a post 5pm espresso; it's after dark when the booming caffeine culture really starts buzzing. It's time to get initiated into some of the country's coolest coffee clubs ...

ESPRESSO SESSIONS

There aren't many gigs where more coffee is drunk than beer, but what else would you expect when Edinburgh's original speciality shop and roastery is hosting the party?

Artisan Roast's popular espresso sessions don't have a fixed timetable or venue; its three cafes across the city host live gigs when opportunities arise, while its Holy Garage pop-up transforms into a fully fledged festival stage when the Fringe comes to town.

'The espresso sessions only became a "thing" about four years ago,' explains Lukasz Gasiorowski of Artisan Roast, *'but we've had live music in the evenings at our Broughton Street venue from the get-go, as a couple of members of the Scottish Chamber Orchestra*

were some of our first customers and used to play all the time.'

What started as impromptu acoustic sets has grown into a regular spot on the Edinburgh Festival Fringe line-up. *'We had about 40 different artists on our stage last year, including bands and some amazing solo artists. And yes, the coffee was still rolling 'til the 4am shut down.*

'We host cupping sessions, espresso masterclasses and trips to the roastery on a regular basis, and these events appeal to the keen coffee connoisseur. Although at the live gigs we'll often get people with no interest in coffee whatsoever wander in after hearing the music. They usually leave as a convert.'

PUMP UP THE JAM

Rising from the ashes of the Glasgow Coffee Jam, the Scottish Coffee Jam was relaunched in 2016 as a monthly collective for the nation's caffeine fiends.

'The original Coffee Jam spawned lifelong friendships, job opportunities, a couple of business deals and even a romance,' explains Ewan Osprey Allan, one of the guys behind the group. *'But the event was small in scale and extremely nerdy – we once compared consistency of hand grinders.'*

Now that the jam is back in action, the brew buffs behind the events have switched things up and are focusing on growing the coffee community with a line-up of inclusive events. Don't sweat, diehards, there are still plenty of opportunities to get geeky. *'I wanted to focus less on the intricate details of coffee and more on the people and the fun stuff,'* says Ewan.

'After a couple of events it became clear that if you want to bring a group of coffee enthusiasts together, you just need to add beer!'

So far there have been a couple of cupping competitions, a latte art throwdown or two, the launch of the Disloyal Seven – a loyalty card encouraging Edinburgh's coffee tourists to try new hangouts – and a welcome-to-the-neighbourhood party for Brew Lab when it opened its second shop. *'Each event has been bigger than the last. We chat, drink and form friendships, irrespective of individual business interests,'* says Ewan.

'The real crux of the events is the idea that in working together, we can improve Scotland's coffee culture.'

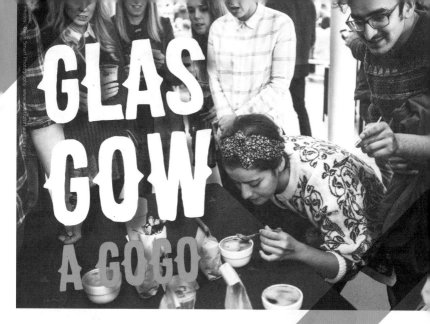

GLASGOW
A GOGO

Meanwhile in Glasgow, Todd Whiteford (pictured) of Glasgow's Avenue Coffee Roasting Co. admits, *'Coffee events can be pretty insular. There's a fine line between encouraging people to take an interest in something pretty niche and making them feel part of what can be a tight gang.'*

And it's creating this inclusive environment for coffee education that Avenue is attempting through its bill of brew events in Scotland's second city. *'We hold brew, espresso and latte art classes all the time and we always encourage participants to come along to our informal latte art smackdowns on a Thursday night. First timers are usually a little nervous but it's pretty chilled and a great first step into Glasgow's coffee community,'* explains Todd.

'FIRST TIMERS ARE USUALLY A LITTLE **NERVOUS**'

'Launching our first coffee beer with Fallen Brewing Co. and holding the Scottish premier of The Coffee Man *film recently was a way to introduce the wider indie community to the speciality scene. We also included a discussion on what's to come in Scottish coffee next year, which was eye opening.'*

TOUR DE SPECIALITY

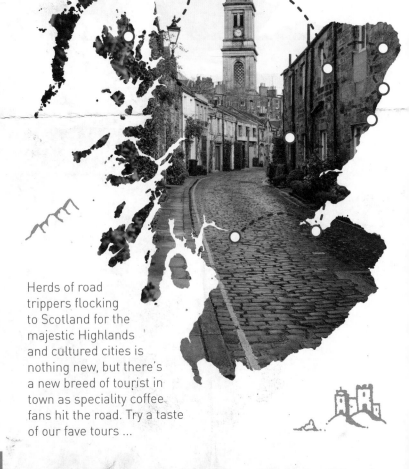

Herds of road trippers flocking to Scotland for the majestic Highlands and cultured cities is nothing new, but there's a new breed of tourist in town as speciality coffee fans hit the road. Try a taste of our fave tours ...

THE HIPSTER TOUR

THE ROUTE Edinburgh or Glasgow – take your pick. Both cities are brimming with brew bars, eclectic coffee shops and indie pop-ups to explore. Just don't forget your checked shirt and beanie.

Kick things off with an early morning flattie among the throng of commuters. Then cafe hop all day through to evening espresso martinis at the latest late night opening.

PACKING ESSENTIALS A notebook in which to jot down new hopper must-haves, plus the phone charger to keep your Instagram followers posted with pourover perfection and a good dose of FOMO.

FUEL THE JOURNEY Brunch is going to be the staple of your diet, whatever the time of day. Expect avo on everything (don't pretend to complain) and more doorstep cheese toasties than you can shake a bottle of sriracha at.

EASE 10/10 No planning required, just grab your *Indy Coffee Guide* and go.

THE NORTHERN TOUR

THE ROUTE Ease into the trip with a caffeinated blast through Aberdeen before skirting around the Cairngorms via Aberfeldy (Habitat Cafe) or Udny (The Coffee Apothecary). Then make a beeline for the Isle of Skye, journeying across the Highlands for ultimate photo ops, with a detour via Ullapool for a coffee stopover (The Ceilidh Place).

PACKING ESSENTIALS If it's a winter trip, take everything warm you've ever owned. Plus an AeroPress, portable grinder and a thermos of hot water – they'll be a lifesaver in the car between venues.

If you're planning a summer jolly, pack a Polaroid camera to catch all the sights and a couple of bottles of cold brew in a cool box.

FUEL THE JOURNEY Steaming bowls of seasonal soup and scones as big as your face are the best way to keep the jitters at bay.

EASE 5/10 You'll need to sort out transport, beds for three or four nights and an itinerary, but hey, satnav is foolproof, Airbnb is cheap and the scenery is definitely worth it.

THE ROASTERY TOUR

THE ROUTE Pay your favourite roasters across the country a visit and have a nosey at what happens to the beans before they reach your cup. An increasing number of roasters are engaging with the public through the introduction of on-site cafes, shops and training facilities. Some, such as Mr Eion in Edinburgh are open to the public the whole time.

PACKING ESSENTIALS Pack light, you're going to need space for all the brewing gear and beans picked up along the way. A pen will also come in handy when you want the rock star roasters to sign your copy of the *Indy Coffee Guide*.

FUEL THE JOURNEY Get one of the roasters to recommend a pukka local pub and replenish the stores with something hearty – man, we loved the roast chicken, haggis bonbons and whisky sauce we had in Stonehaven during our trip.

EASE 7/10 Check out the roasters at the back of the guide to find those you can visit. Some aren't open to the public, but if you ping them a quick tweet, who knows? They're a friendly bunch.

~ FROM ~
LATTE
TO
LANDFILL

Can speciality coffee go hand in hand with sustainability?

We asked eco campaigner **Hugh Fearnley-Whittingstall** and reusable pioneers **KeepCup** if the indies can help reduce the number of coffee cups ending up in landfill by leading the way ...

'PEOPLE SHOULD FEEL NO SHAME IN BRINGING THEIR OWN CONTAINERS WITH THEM'

Coffee addicts are responsible for a mountain of toxic waste that's ending up in landfill. It's estimated that in the UK alone, coffee drinkers get through around 2.5 billion disposable cups per year – and only one in a thousand of these is currently recycled.

The situation is utterly *'untenable'* according to KeepCup's co-founder Abigail Forsyth.

'It demonstrates the catastrophic impact of convenience culture on the planet,' says the Aussie entrepreneur, who in 2008 hit upon the idea of creating reusable cups for the coffee-to-go crowd.

It's just one of the many eco-friendly initiatives that have been welcomed across the speciality scene; others include discounts for drinkers who bring their own reusables and the take up of fully compostable cups in many indie cafes.

In mainland Europe, quirky ideas like the Freiburg Cup have seen customers buying their coffee in a reusable, only to drop off the cup later at a different cafe for someone else to use.

'Giving people "permission" to reuse, by providing a small discount, or advertising that reusables are welcome, is critical if you want to create behaviour change,' says Abigail, who finds the UK speciality scene, with its emphasis on coffee provenance and integrity, particularly welcoming to innovations like KeepCup.

2.5 BILLION
DISPOSABLE CUPS PER YEAR

Creating a stylish and practical product that coffee lovers would remember to reuse was key to the company's success: the barista-standard cups are not only lightweight, unbreakable and easy to clean, but can also be customised in bright colours.

'We knew that to get repeat use, KeepCup needed to be a product that customers would enjoy using,' she says.

Blaming the mountains of coffee cups ending up in landfill solely on non-recyclables is almost certainly over simplifying the issue. Many coffee cups are recyclable, but have plastic linings which aren't. The problem is not the cups themselves but the lack of recycling facilities to separate out the constituent parts.

One campaigner who has done much to lift the lid on this problem is Hugh Fearnley-Whittingstall, who believes indie coffee shops can do their bit in the fight for a sustainable future.

'Independents can blaze a trail and show the big name retailers that it can be done,' says Hugh.

He favours compostable cups or investigating the likes of Frugalpac, which unlike many so-called "recyclable" coffee cups can be disposed of through the normal paper stream at the recycling centre.

And in terms of the coffee itself, he recommends searching out companies such as bio-bean which recycle waste coffee grounds into all kinds of useful biofuels.

'MANY COFFEE CUPS ARE RECYCLABLE, BUT HAVE **PLASTIC LININGS** WHICH AREN'T'

Of course, coffee isn't the only culprit when it comes to cafe waste. *'Doggy bags are a must in a responsible cafe,'* says Hugh who is a fan of compostable containers like Vegware. *'You never know quite how hungry your diners are going to be and you always want to err on the side of being generous. Every restaurant should make it easy for people to take extra food home with them. If customers can do that in a sustainable, reusable container, so much the better. I think people should feel no shame in bringing their own containers with them.'*

KeepCup's Abigail hopes that when it comes to coffee, speciality and sustainability will go hand in hand.

'As a crop very sensitive to altitude and climate, coffee is seriously impacted by climate change. It makes little sense to do something at one end of the chain that ends up destroying the source.'

And Scotland, believes Glasgow-born Abigail, is a shining beacon for the cause.

'Scotland should be enormously proud of its renewable energy impact, a great example to the world and hope for the future. Gaun yersel Scotland!'

DEFINING SPECIALITY

A definition of speciality coffee is a much chewed over topic among coffee geeks and industry specialists. We asked African-coffee importer, **Phil Schluter** for his take on the issue

In 2003, I sat with a group of like-minded coffee professionals at the International Coffee Organisation (ICO) in London to found the Speciality Coffee Association of Europe (SCAE). At the time, we had many discussions as to what defined speciality coffee. From the Italians who loved their espresso and were happy to include some good robustas, to the Norwegians who would not dream of buying robusta and preferred other brew methods, we united around a common goal to build a network of people enthusiastic about speciality.

With the recent merger of the SCAA in America, with the SCAE, I have been reflecting again on what it is that defines us. I don't presume to have the answer, but I think we could start the conversation around the following.

We...

Value quality and passion over price and convenience

Take interest in, and seek to understand the journey our beans make, from seed to sip

Create a working environment to be enjoyed, not endured

Inherently build sustainability through generating a significant and tangible added value

Are a potent force for change: the passion we invest creates huge value which can be fairly shared

Make decisions with all our senses

Actively seek out the unique and remarkable and enjoy sharing it with others

WHAT DO YOU THINK?
🐦 JOIN THE CONVERSATION ON TWITTER 🐦
#DEFININGSPECIALITYCOFFEE

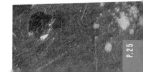

TAKING THE Q

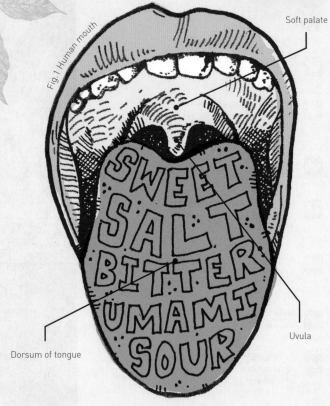

Fig.1 Human mouth

Soft palate

SWEET
SALT
BITTER
UMAMI
SOUR

Dorsum of tongue

Uvula

The term **"Q grader"** is bandied about in the world of speciality coffee, but what does it mean? **John Thompson** of **Coffee Nexus** in Edinburgh should know – he is one – and explains why coffee lovers across the world have learned to mind their beans and Qs

C ould you identify the 36 scents found in coffee? Would you be able to faultlessly grade beans for their quality? Are you able to detect sweet, salty and sour tastes in your favourite brew?

These are just the kinds of challenging olfactory and sensory skills that even the most experienced coffee connoisseur must demonstrate to become a Q grader.

The Q system was set up to enable coffee experts around the globe to speak the same lingo when it comes to deciding what is and what isn't Q grade coffee. That is, coffee that's good enough to score 80 or above on the Speciality Coffee Association (SCA) cupping form – more on that later.

'The core concept of the Q system is that it creates a shared understanding of coffee quality within the supply chain, from producer to end user,' says John, who at Nexus carries out consultancy, training and testing for the coffee industry. 'Underpinning this is a set of standards, methodologies and language, because if cuppers can calibrate quality globally, it's possible to have a dialogue and shared vision of how to improve coffee over time.'

TESTING TIMES

To ensure coffee is scored in a consistent way, Q graders use a standard cupping form from the Speciality Coffee Association (SCA) for arabica beans and the Ugandan Coffee Development Authority (UCDA) form for robusta. To fill it out accurately, however, the graders need razor sharp sensory skills, which is where intense training comes in. 'After three days of training, you have to undertake a series of tests to ascertain your consistency and the ability to recognise quality,' says John, who is not only a Q grader for arabica beans but also recently passed his robusta exams, making him the first R grader in Scotland - and one of only three in the UK (there are less than 10 in Europe).

'COULD YOU IDENTIFY THE **36 SCENTS** FOUND IN COFFEE?'

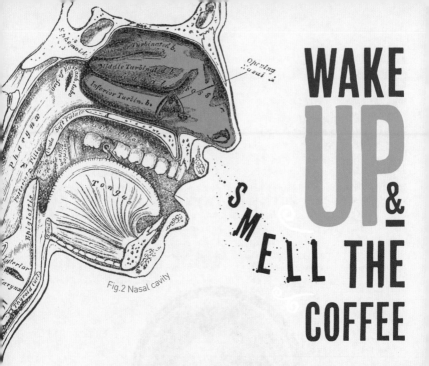

Fig.2 Nasal cavity

WAKE UP & SMELL THE COFFEE

... AND RELAX

Honing a sense of smell is one of the vital skills for a Q grader, so the olfactory tests check the ability to recognise key odours.

'Part of the trick to passing is to stay relaxed because, as with all sensory analysis, the more relaxed you are, the more focused you'll be,' says John.

'There are four different aroma groups. Those you're more likely to detect in speciality coffee are the enzymatic aromas (floral, fruit) and sugar browning aromas (nuttiness, caramel and cocoa).'

SWEET · SALT · BITTER · SOUR · UMAMI

'UNDERSTANDING WHAT SOURNESS OR SWEETNESS IS IN SOLUTION, WITHOUT THE NOISE OF FLAVOUR'

SENSORY OVERLOAD

The trickiest assessment, though, is rumoured to be the sensory skills test. *'A lot of people get worried about the test to see if you can differentiate between sweet, salt, bitter and sour, but it's such a useful skill for identifying the difference between coffees.*

'Understanding what sourness or sweetness is in solution, without the noise of flavour, helps when you start assessing coffee objectively.'

Tests also include assessments in triangulations (spotting the odd one out in a set of coffees), cupping and the physical grading of coffee which involves identifying its physical defects.

'The triangulation tests are very useful – I use the same method when developing roast profiles with clients – because it encourages you to check if you can consistently spot a difference between two coffees.

'The cupping test assesses if you can use the SCA cupping form consistently by rewarding quality and scoring poor coffees appropriately.'

THE Q-TEAM

As the most exacting sensory coffee course on the planet, the few who pass all the tests get to join an elite group of super tasters - of which there are only around 3,500 worldwide.

S30

Perfect Touch

 Wide beverage menu

 Self adjusting grinders

 Bi-directional Wi-Fi control

LaCimbali **S30** is the new superautomatic machine created to offer up to **24 different recipes**. The grouphead design guarantees maximum reliability and consistent beverage quality, while the new milk circuit delivers hot and cold frothed milk directly to the cup.
LaCimbali **S30**, the perfect way to satisfy every taste.

reddot award 2016
winner

PILGRIMS COFFEE HOUSE
№ 54

YOUR JOURNEY STARTS HERE

CAFES

Coffee shops and cafes where you can drink
top-notch speciality coffee. We've split the whole
of Scotland into areas to help you find places
near you.

ROASTERS

Meet the leading speciality coffee roasters in
Scotland and discover where to source beans to
use at home.

Finally, you'll discover More Good Cups and More
Good Roasters at the end of each section.

MAPS

Every cafe and roaster has a number so you can
find them either on the area map at the start
of each section, or on the detailed city maps of
Glasgow and Edinburgh.

**Don't forget to let us know how you get on as you
explore the best speciality cafes and roasters:**

www.indycoffee.guide

🐦 @indycoffeeguide 📷 @indycoffeeguide

MAPS

KEY

Cafe

Roaster

More Good Cups

More Good Roasters

Coffee Training Facility

SCOTLAND BY AREA

To make it easier for you to find cafes and roasters, we've split up Scotland into four areas

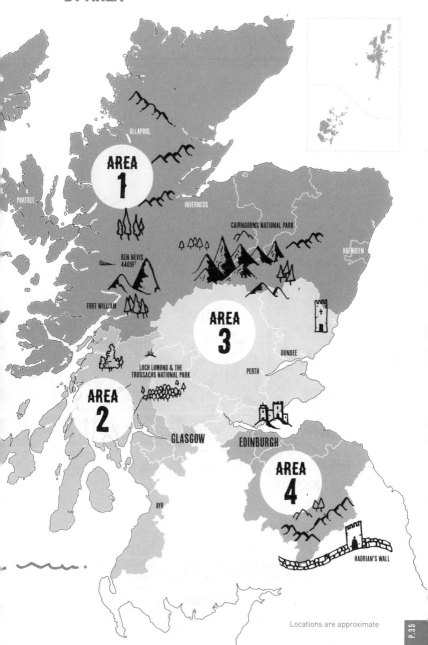

Locations are approximate

CAIRNGORM COFFEE
№33

CAFES

AREA 1

RED ROOF CAFE
№ 2

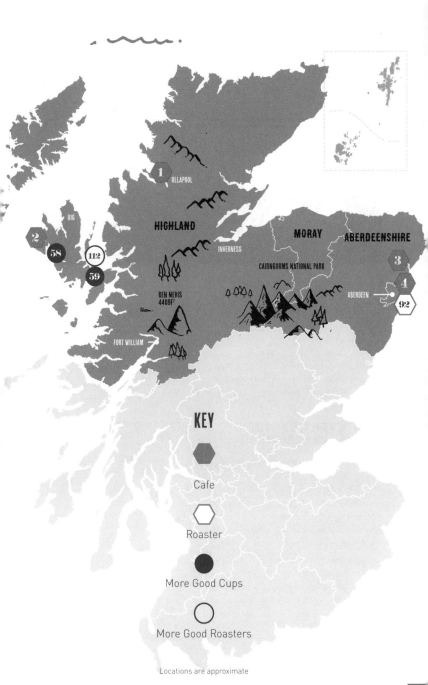

HIGHLAND

MORAY

ABERDEENSHIRE

ULLAPOOL

UIG

INVERNESS

CAIRNGORMS NATIONAL PARK

BEN NEVIS
4409FT

ABERDEEN

FORT WILLIAM

1

2

58

112

59

3

4

92

KEY

Cafe

Roaster

More Good Cups

More Good Roasters

Locations are approximate

1. THE CEILIDH PLACE

12-14 West Argyle Street, Ullapool, Ross-shire, IV26 2TY.

It may be cold outside (this is pretty far north) but the fire is usually lit and you're always guaranteed a steaming, quality cup of Glen Lyon and a warm welcome at The Ceilidh Place.

At the heart of this arty hotel is the cafe bar where espresso based coffees remain on the go, day into evening. It's here that head chef Scott Morrison creates flavour packed dishes from local ingredients – think fish from the pier, tatties from the lochside and herbs picked in the garden.

INSIDER'S TIP THE HOTEL IS FAMOUS FOR ITS AWESOME HOGMANAY PARTY

Due to its position on the stunning 500-mile coastal road (North Coast 500), which stretches around the tip of Scotland, it's not just coffee lovers who've put the hotel high on the hit list. With its refurbished music venue and eclectic bookshop, it's also a must for those seeking original beats and offbeat books in an off-the-beaten-track Highlands setting.

'We want The Ceilidh Place to be good for the soul,' says owner Rebecca Urquhart, whose father, the actor Robert Urquhart first opened a small cafe on the site in 1970 with the intention of it becoming a happening hub for those who like to eat, meet, sing and chat.

KEY ROASTER
Glen Lyon
Coffee Roasters

BREWING METHOD
Espresso

MACHINE
Gaggia

GRINDER
Mahlkonig EK 30

OPENING HOURS
Mon-Sun
8am-11pm

www.theceilidhplace.com   T: 01854 612103

f The Ceilidh Place   🐦 @theceilidhplace   📷 @1970ceil

MAP Nº 2. RED ROOF CAFE

Holmisdale, Glendale, Isle of Skye, IV55 8WS.

Perched on the side of a hill and reached along a network of coiling country roads, Red Roof Cafe on the Isle of Skye must be one of the UK's most remote speciality spots. However, award winning organic grub and carefully crafted coffee certainly warrant a hike to this hippy hangout.

Owners Gareth and Iona Craft haven't let their rural location impede their environmental ethic, stocking the larder with local produce, cooking homegrowns in the kitchen and sourcing beans with provenance from Workshop Coffee.

INSIDER'S TIP
MAKE SURE TO CHECK RED ROOF'S WEBSITE FOR SEASONAL OPENING HOURS BEFORE AN EXPEDITION

The crab and lobster caught just down the road are a regular feature on the daily specials menu and you can thank the brood of hens you passed on the way in for their role in the slice of homemade cake that'll follow lunch.

Just as the specials change with the seasons, so do the beans in the hopper, reflecting the seasonal coffee harvest. Workshop's handiwork is available as espresso, V60 and french press, alongside an impressive collection of speciality teas.

KEY ROASTER
Workshop Coffee

BREWING METHODS
Espresso, V60, french press

MACHINE
1000espressos

GRINDER
Mahlkonig EK 43

OPENING HOURS
Seasonal

www.redroofskye.co.uk   T: 01470 511766

f Red Roof Cafe Gallery   🐦 @redroofskye   📷 @redroofskye

MAP 3. THE COFFEE APOTHECARY

Udny, Ellon, Aberdeenshire, AB41 7PQ.

After marrying in Edinburgh, Jonny and Ali Aspden shot off on a three year round-the-world adventure during which they tried so many interesting and crazy flavours – and a couple of incredible cups of coffee – that the pair fell in love with the idea of running their own cafe.

So, on returning to Scotland, they took over an old rural post office in Aberdeenshire, which they named The Coffee Apothecary, unaware that there had once been a pharmacy on the site.

Armed with power tools and a lot of imagination, they set about giving upcycled objects a new lease of life (don't leave without checking out the penny floor in the toilets), making the cafe a fascinating place to while away an afternoon over an espresso or filter, with a scrumptious fresh-from-the-oven cake.

INSIDER'S TIP LOOK OUT FOR EVENING EVENTS WITH WINE AND CRAFT BEER

A tempting lunch menu draws on local organic veg and free range meats to offer dishes from goat curry to beef tacos, while those luxuriating in the speciality brews remark on the quality of the coffee, sourced from Edinburgh's Artisan Roast.

KEY ROASTER
Artisan Roast
Coffee Roasters

BREWING METHODS
Espresso, Kalita
Wave, french press

MACHINES
La Marzocco Linea
PB ABR, Marco SP9

GRINDERS
Mahlkonig K30,
Mahlkonig EK 43

OPENING HOURS
Mon-Sat
9am-4pm

www.thecoffeeapothecary.co.uk   T: 01651 842253

f The Coffee Apothecary   🐦 @udnyapothecary   📷 @thecoffeeapothecary

MAP N° 4. FOODSTORY

13-15 Thistle Street, Aberdeen, AB10 1XZ.

In the year since the first guide hit the Scottish speciality scene, Sandy and Lara – the green duo behind Aberdeen's ethical community cafe – have been busy building the Foodstory brand.

The pair have recently also acquired the building next door and have plans to expand the kitchen, meaning even more of that locally sourced, veggie and organic grub that Foodstory is famed for – as well as extra space for the throng of locals to catch up over the quality coffee offering.

INSIDER'S TIP LOOK OUT FOR FOODSTORY MARK II, A CONVERTED HORSE BOX HITTING THE STREETS OF ABERDEEN SOON

The super friendly gaggle of baristas continue to serve Aberdeen's caffeine fans with an expanding menu of espresso and filter options from a broad repertoire of Scottish roasters.

Browse the bi-monthly, rotating filter board, looking out for appearances from a wide variety of guest roasters such as Sundlaug and Steampunk, before pairing your pick with something tasty from the seasonal menu or one of the incredible edibles on the cake stand.

KEY ROASTER
Dear Green
Coffee Roasters

BREWING METHODS
Espresso, V60,
AeroPress, Chemex

MACHINE
La Marzocco
Linea

GRINDERS
Mazzer Kold,
Mahlkonig Tanzania

OPENING HOURS
Mon-Thu 8am-9pm
Fri 8am-10pm
Sat 9am-9pm

Gluten FREE

COFFEE BEANS AVAILABLE

ALTERNATIVE MILK

WIFI

FAMILY FRIENDLY

BRING YOUR OWN Cup.

www.foodstorycafe.co.uk

f Foodstory   🐦 @foodstorycoffee   📷 @foodstoryscotland

REUSERS GUIDE

WASH YOUR KEEPCUP
KEEP IT CLEAN
KEEP IT UPRIGHT
HAND OVER THE CUP
KEEP YOUR LID

RINSE QUICKLY
REMEMBER IT
KEEP IN YOUR BAG. CAR OR DESK.

VOTE WITH YOUR FEET.
BUY ONCE. BUY WELL.

COMPOST.
DRINK FROM THE TAP

REUSE OR REFRAIN

AREA 2

FOR FIKA SAKE
№ 8

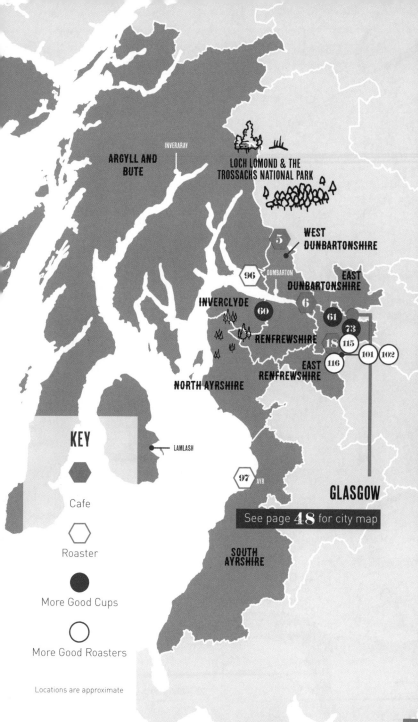

ARGYLL AND
BUTE

INVERARAY

LOCH LOMOND & THE
TROSSACHS NATIONAL PARK

WEST
DUNBARTONSHIRE

5

96   DUMBARTON

EAST
DUNBARTONSHIRE

INVERCLYDE   60   6

61   73

RENFREWSHIRE   18   115

EAST   101   102
RENFREWSHIRE   116

NORTH AYRSHIRE

KEY

LAMLASH

97   AYR

GLASGOW

See page 48 for city map

Cafe

Roaster

SOUTH
AYRSHIRE

More Good Cups

More Good Roasters

Locations are approximate

P.47

GLASGOW CITY CENTRE

Locations are approximate

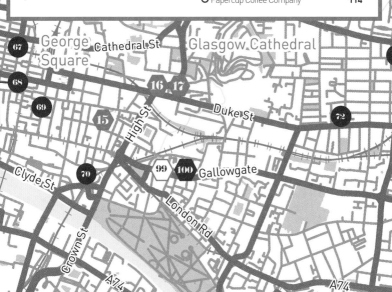

№5. ST MOCHA COFFEE SHOP AND ICE CREAM PARLOUR

Main Street, Balmaha, Loch Lomond, Glasgow, G63 0JQ.

Loch Lomond's first speciality spot may neighbour the picturesque West Highland Way but it's the ingenious use of machine parts around the shop – check out the portafilter door handles and the grinder blades in the loos – that'll keep coffee geeks happy.

In the grinders that survived the designer's purge, you'll find St Mocha's own blend from Glasgow's Dear Green, as well as a guest from a rotating line-up of Scottish roasters such as Charlie Mills.

INSIDER'S TIP IN SUMMER, HOP ON A BOAT ACROSS LOCH LOMOND AND PAY A VISIT TO ST MOCHA'S SECOND VENUE ON LUSS PIER

Homemade ice cream – Loch Lomond's first – is the guys' other speciality. A couple of scoops of wild strawberry or pistachio should keep the kids quiet while you savour a silky shot of espresso poured over vanilla. There's also a good selection of seasonal soups and cakes if you're after something more substantial.

And we can recommend the comfy lodgings next door at the award winning Oak Tree Inn which are perfectly positioned for coffee tourists seeking speciality in this neck of the woods.

KEY ROASTER
Dear Green
Coffee Roasters

BREWING METHOD
Espresso

MACHINE
La Marzocco
Linea

GRINDER
Mazzer Kold

OPENING HOURS
Mon-Sun
10am-5pm
Extended hours
in summer

Gluten FREE · COFFEE BEANS AVAILABLE · ALTERNATIVE MILK · WIFI · CYCLE FRIENDLY · OUTDOOR SEATING · FAMILY FRIENDLY · DISABLED ACCESS · BRING YOUR OWN CUP

---

www.stmocha.co.uk   T: 01360 870492

f St Mocha Coffee Shop & Ice Cream Parlour   🐦 @stmochacoffee   📷 @stmochacoffee

^{MAP №}6. GRACE & FAVOUR

11 Roman Road, Bearsden, Glasgow, G61 2SR.

Grace & Favour is a lovely place to be. All cosy lighting, home baking, warm welcome and good coffee made with speciality beans.

With everything baked in-house, you won't be happy with just a Home Ground Coffee, however beautifully it is served as espresso or AeroPress. Rhubarb meringue pies, whopping cheese scones and mini bakewell tarts mark the passing seasons in melt-in-the-mouth splendour.

The interior has enjoyed a wee makeover since last year's guide, though the antlers are still going strong and add a Highlands flavour to this urban cafe in suburban Glasgow.

INSIDER'S TIP COMBINE YOUR VISIT WITH A TRIP TO THE SECOND CENTURY ROMAN BATH HOUSE, 100 YARDS AWAY

Also new this year is the addition of dinner on Friday and Saturday nights. The chefs have already won a legion of local fans who visit for cracking breakfasts, gourmet lunches and delicious cakes, so it's no surprise to find the evening events fully booked and hugely successful.

KEY ROASTER
Home Ground Coffee

BREWING METHODS
Espresso, AeroPress

MACHINE
La Marzocco

GRINDERS
Fiorenzato, Mazzer Jolly

OPENING HOURS
Mon-Sat
8.30am-5pm
Fri-Sat 6pm-11pm
Sun 9am-5pm

 Gluten FREE

 COFFEE BEANS AVAILABLE

 ALTERNATIVE MILK

 WIFI

 OUTDOOR seating

 FAMILY FRIENDLY

www.graceandfavourcoffee.com T: 01415 706501

f Grace & Favour 📷 @graceandfavourcoffee

7. IT ALL STARTED HERE

Pop up at events throughout Glasgow and central Scotland.

Coffee fans will want to check out William Heenan's mobile speciality stall, a regular Glasgow fixture at Partick Farmers' Market and bakery47.

You'll also find his popular pop-up at events as diverse as Piping Live (the world bagpipe championships) and Eaglesham Beer Festival (where he's now a legend for a mean coffee cocktail created with a natural yirgacheffe).

'We pop up anywhere that needs good coffee,' says William, who has a penchant for a fruity brew.

'If it's fruity, we're all over it. Getting blueberry or strawberry notes in an espresso or flat white can be new to customers who are used to drinking blends, but I want to show how diverse coffee can taste. And people are a lot more receptive than you might think.'

INSIDER'S TIP
LOOK OUT FOR TOP UK AND EUROPEAN GUEST ROASTERS ON THE MENU

Working with Foundry Coffee, William has found his ideal roaster which enables him to take roasted, naturally processed beans and turn them into espresso with a winning combination of acidity and sweetness.

'As one of our roasters said, "coffee is a fruit – so don't let the fruitiness scare you".'

KEY ROASTER
Foundry Coffee Roasters

BREWING METHODS
Espresso, batch brew

MACHINE
Rancilio Classe 6

GRINDERS
Mythos One
Clima Pro,
Mahlkonig EK 43

OPENING HOURS
Varies by location
Check social media

www.allstartedhere.wordpress.com   T: 07743 069632

f It All Started Here   🐦 @allstartedhere   📷 @allstartedherecoffee

MAP N° 8. FOR FIKA SAKE

7 Keith Street, Glasgow, G11 6QQ.

With customers bashing out tunes on the free-for-all piano, kids giggling in the den, architects working on the first floor and local musos holding jamming sessions, For Fika Sake is a refreshingly inclusive experience.

Launched as a community interest cafe at the start of 2016, it's not aligned to any organisation but simply exists to provide great coffee and a space for the community. So everyone is welcome – from parents with toddlers to the elderly (the cafe is a Dementia Friend).

INSIDER'S TIP TRY SCANDI-STYLE BAKES FOR YOUR FIKA BREAK

Proprietor Simon is a photographer and his creativity comes through in spades – from the Friday night jam sessions to the Barter and Band swap meets.

The good vibes are kept buzzin' by Dear Green's Rwandan blend as the house roast, which is served as espresso based drinks and as V60, Chemex and AeroPress. There's an emphasis on encouraging customers to try their coffee in different ways, with guest roasts also on the agenda.

KEY ROASTER
Dear Green
Coffee Roasters

BREWING METHODS
Espresso, V60, AeroPress, Chemex, cold brew

MACHINE
La Marzocco Linea

GRINDER
Mazzer Super Jolly

OPENING HOURS
Mon-Wed
9am-5pm
Thu-Fri
9am-6pm
Sat 9am-5pm
Sun 10am-5pm
Extended hours in summer

 Gluten FREE

 ALTERNATIVE MILK

 WIFI

 CYCLE FRIENDLY

 FAMILY FRIENDLY

 DISABLED ACCESS

 BRING YOUR OWN CUP

www.forfikasake.com   T: 07851 255804

f For Fika Sake   🐦 @forfikasake   📷 @forfikasake

№9. KEMBER & JONES

134 Byres Road, Glasgow, G12 8TD.

We'd advise that you steer clear of Kember & Jones if you're trying to exercise any kind of calorific self control, as its counter of homemade pistachio and rosewater cake, mountainous meringues and dainty pastel macarons will sink all good intentions.

The coffee is just as good – all roasted on its new 5kg Probat and featuring single origins and espresso blends – as is the extensive range of breads from the Kember & Jones bakery.

INSIDER'S TIP VISIT IN THE EVENING FOR BIG BOWLS OF CHEERFULLY HEARTY SPECIALS

As you may have sussed, this is not your average coffee shop, rather, it's an emporium of good things of the gastronomic variety. Deli delights, shelves groaning with grocery store faves, rare roast beef baguettes with swiss cheese and rocket, plus wines and craft beers are all served until late in a groovy West End location. It ticks all the boxes.

The hot choc is notable too – throw caution to the wind and go wild with a chilli spiked Aztec or melt into a hot white chocolate with cardamom and cinnamon.

KEY ROASTER
Kember & Jones

BREWING METHOD
Espresso

MACHINE
La Marzocco Linea

GRINDER
Mahlkonig K30

OPENING HOURS
Mon-Fri 8am-10pm
Sat 9am-10pm
Sun 9am-6pm

 Gluten FREE

 COFFEE BEANS AVAILABLE

 ALTERNATIVE MILK

 WIFI

 CYCLE FRIENDLY

 OUTDOOR seating

FAMILY FRIENDLY

DISABLED ACCESS

---

www.kemberandjones.co.uk   T: 01413 373851

f Kember & Jones   🐦 @kemberandjones   📷 @kemberandjones

MAP 10. AVENUE COFFEE - BYRES ROAD

291 Byres Road, Glasgow, G12 8TL.

A shot of buttered bulletproof coffee is just one of the weird and wonderful kicks to be had at Avenue. And that's not the extent of the unconventional at the roaster's first cafe in Glasgow – not by half.

If your flat white has you feeling deflated, pep up your day with a turmeric latte. Once past the curiously thick consistency, the warming spices and purported health benefits make it an attractive proposition. Or there's the cherry hot chocolate with homemade maraschino syrup and almond milk.

INSIDER'S TIP GET HERE EARLY ON WEEKENDS TO BEAT THE CROWDS OF CAFFEINE CONVERTS

However, it's the coffee purists who are best provided for, with Avenue's own-roasted range of single origins that go on the board (with notes) as the global coffee seasons change. Start with the Skyscraper house blend and follow wherever your fancy takes you.

KEY ROASTER
Avenue Coffee Roasting Co.

BREWING METHODS
Espresso, AeroPress

MACHINE
Sanremo Verona RS

GRINDER
Mahlkonig K30

OPENING HOURS
Mon-Sun
8.30am-7pm

Gluten FREE

COFFEE BEANS AVAILABLE

ALTERNATIVE MILK

WIFI

OUTDOOR SEATING

COFFEE COURSES AVAILABLE

FAMILY FRIENDLY

DISABLED ACCESS

BRING YOUR OWN Cup

www.avenue.coffee   T: 01413 395336

f Avenue Coffee   🐦 @avenue_coffee   📷 @avenuecoffeeglasgow

MAP No. 11. PAPERCUP COFFEE COMPANY – GREAT WESTERN ROAD

603 Great Western Road, Glasgow, G12 8HX.

One of a clutch of unique, indie coffee finds on the Great Western Road in Glasgow's West End, Papercup is a quirky, arty little hot spot of coffee cool. And one that's definitely worth hunting out.

Sourcing and roasting coffee since 2012, the team is understandably serious about providing a high quality caffeinated experience, so beans can be imbibed as espresso (and a stonking flat white), V60 and AeroPress as well as cold brew. You'll also find beans from the best roasters around the world on the brew bar, which mixes things up a little.

INSIDER'S TIP: GET TO GRIPS WITH LATTE ART AT PAPERCUP'S CLASSES

The creativity continues in the diverse brunch menu with dishes such as rhubarb and custard french toast and a whole load of homebakes – including drop-dead gorgeous salted caramel and peanut butter cookies. To top it off, Papercup has just launched a coffee chocolate bar and, for the budding barista, there are free cuppings and coffee training sessions.

With a huge coffee inspired mural on the main wall, strings of lights and vintage styling, its cup runneth over.

KEY ROASTER
Papercup Coffee Company

BREWING METHODS
Espresso, V60, AeroPress, cold brew

MACHINE
La Marzocco Linea Custom

GRINDERS
Mythos, Ditting, Mazzer Robur

OPENING HOURS
Mon-Fri
8.30am-6pm
Sat-Sun
9am-5.30pm

 Gluten FREE

 COFFEE BEANS AVAILABLE

 ALTERNATIVE MILK

 WIFI

 CYCLE FRIENDLY

 OUTDOOR SEATING

 COFFEE COURSES AVAILABLE

 FAMILY FRIENDLY

 DISABLED ACCESS

BRING YOUR OWN Cup

www.papercupcoffee.co.uk   T: 07719 454376

f Papercup Coffee Company   🐦 @pccoffeeuk   📷 @pccoffeeuk

HOSTED BY

Dear
GREEN
Coffee Roasters

GLASGOW
COFFEE
FESTIVAL

THE BRIGGAIT, GLASGOW
6-7 May 2017

We are excited to be part of a **growing specialty coffee culture in Scotland** and are celebrating this vibrant scene in an all-encompassing two-day event showcasing the passion for quality coffee in our Scottish coffee community.

The festival will feature a multitude of coffee contributors, exhibitors, masterclasses, workshops, presentations and demonstrations.

PLUS: The event will be hosting the **SCA UK Brewers Cup** and the **UK Barista Championship Scottish Heat.**

The Briggait | 141 Bridgegate | Glasgow | G1 5HZ

f GlasgowCoffeeFestival 🐦 glascoffeefest 📷 Glasgowcoffeefestival

12. ARTISAN ROAST - GIBSON STREET

15-17 Gibson Street, Glasgow, G12 8NU.

Located in one of the West End's most vibrant and community spirited streets is the Glaswegian hub of Artisan Roast. As the first speciality coffee shop in Glasgow, this cosy, arty rendezvous still offers one of the most sought-after cups in Scotland.

With coffee from its Edinburgh roastery sent through daily, the brew bar is always exciting. As coffee roasters, Artisan has an ever-changing selection of five to ten coffees from around the world on the go. Ask the baristas what they would recommend as espresso or your brew choice, via V60, Chemex, AeroPress or cafetiere. They'll even talk you through the brewing methods so you can replicate it all at home.

INSIDER'S TIP SIGN UP FOR ARTISAN'S MASTERCLASS TO PERFECT YOUR ESPRESSO

Yet what makes the Glasgow shop special among the Artisan Roast family is its kitchen, where the chefs indulge their passion for delicious food to complement the award winning coffees.

The cafe focuses on local, organic, vegan and gluten-free delights for breakfast, lunch and afternoon treats – all baked in-house, naturally.

KEY ROASTER
Artisan Roast Coffee Roasters

BREWING METHODS
Espresso, V60, AeroPress, Chemex, cafetiere

MACHINE
La Marzocco GB5

GRINDERS
Mazzer Major Electronic, Mahlkonig K30

OPENING HOURS
Mon-Thu
8am-7pm
Fri 8am-6.30pm
Sat-Sun
9am-6.30pm

 Gluten FREE

 COFFEE BEANS AVAILABLE

 ALTERNATIVE MILK

 WIFI

 OUTDOOR Seating

 COFFEE COURSES AVAILABLE

 FAMILY friendly

 DISABLED ACCESS

BRING YOUR OWN Cup.

www.artisanroast.co.uk   T: 07864 984253

f Artisan Roast Glasgow   🐦 @artisanroastgla   📷 @artisan_roast_glasgow

13. AVENUE COFFEE

321 Great Western Road, Glasgow, G4 9HR.

With espresso, Chemex, AeroPress, Kalita Wave, french press and V60 on offer, this is a stimulating place to drink speciality coffee in Glasgow. And when you discover that all of the coffee served is roasted upstairs, you know you're onto something good.

It's easy to blow a day's caffeine allowance in just one visit. Generally, three different coffees are available for filter, alongside an espresso roast – with notes explaining all of their flavour profiles.

INSIDER'S TIP
TRY THE AVENUE X FALLEN BREWERY PALE ALE MASHUP, AND LOOK OUT FOR UPCOMING COFFEE COCKTAILS TOO

The space itself is simple and contemporary, brought to life with the hiss of the steam wand and the sizzle of bacon behind the counter.

The choice of edibles is as wide as the coffee choice and especially scrummy are the breakfast dishes such as porridge with coconut milk, mango, papaya, nutmeg and maple syrup. Or try the eggs en cocotte (all Scottish, free range and organic) with Stornaway black pudding. Then come back for lunch and finish with an affogato or a coffee tonic.

KEY ROASTER
Avenue Coffee
Roasting Co.

BREWING METHODS
Espresso, V60,
AeroPress, Chemex,
Kalita Wave,
french press

MACHINE
Sanremo Opera

GRINDERS
Mythos One,
Mahlkonig K30

OPENING HOURS
Mon-Tue
9.30am-5pm
Wed-Sun
9.30am-6pm

 Gluten FREE

 COFFEE BEANS AVAILABLE

 ALTE RNA TIVE MILK

 WIFI

 OUTDOOR seating

 COFFEE COURSES AVAILABLE

 FAMILY FRIENDLY

 BRING YOUR OWN cup

www.avenue.coffee   T: 01413 391334

f Avenue Coffee 🐦 @avenue_coffee @ @avenuecoffeeglasgow

MAP Nº 14. PRIMAL ROAST

278 St Vincent Street, Glasgow, G2 5RL.

As senior sous at Glasgow's much loved Ubiquitous Chip for five years, and a chef for 18, Iain Walker was well acquainted with fine dining. But finding himself increasingly drawn to clean eating, along with an interest in the benefits of coffee, Iain's interests eventually evolved into the setting up of Primal Roast.

His first solo venture, the site is surprisingly roomy (the basement site hides another dining area out back) and is fast becoming Glasgow's go-to spot for a happy mashup of speciality coffee and healthy eating.

Visit for a breakfast of steaming porridge with banana, berries and nut butter or a superfood breakfast bar, while lunch is all about the Buddha bowls of fluffy rice with slow cooked meat or veg and homemade relish.

INSIDER'S TIP LOOK OUT FOR A BURGEONING CALENDAR OF CUPPING AND COFFEE EVENTS

In fact everything is made on site, from the soups to the bakes and much of it is vegan, as well as refined sugar and dairy-free. That's not to say you can't have cow's milk in your coffee, but there are plenty of alternatives. The house roast comes courtesy of Dear Green and there's a rotating menu of guest beans.

KEY ROASTER
Dear Green Coffee Roasters

BREWING METHODS
Espresso, V60, AeroPress

MACHINE
La Marzocco Linea

GRINDERS
Mazzer Super Jolly, Baratza Encore

OPENING HOURS
Mon-Fri
7.30am-4pm
Sat 10am-3pm

Gluten FREE / COFFEE BEANS AVAILABLE / ALTERNATIVE MILK / WIFI / OUTDOOR SEATING / FAMILY FRIENDLY

www.primalroast.com T: 01412 222750

f Primal Roast 🐦 @primalroast 📷 @primalroast

15. SPITFIRE

127 Candleriggs, Merchant City, Glasgow, G1 1NP.

Photos: Gavin Smart Photography www.viewfromtheoutside.net

It's been a busy second year at Glasgow's funky, Fifties inspired Spitfire Espresso as owners Danny and Emily have added having a baby (who arrived rather earlier than expected) and buying a house, to the business of running the cafe.

Kiwi Danny's as chipper as ever though, and his cheerful vibe permeates the diner-style cafe as buzzily as the rare 1950s rockabilly tunes and the hiss of the La Marzocco coffee machine.

INSIDER'S TIP WANT SOMETHING STRONGER? CHECK OUT THE CRAFT BEER AND WINE LIST

Glasgow's Avenue Coffee has hand-crafted Spitfire's bespoke Gunnerbeans blend, which is a mix of Colombian beans, with a touch of Brazilian to add a chocolate note. It's served with a luscious non-homogenised milk from a single farm in Ayrshire.

At breakfast the wartime theme continues with dishes such as the Hawker Hurricane of homemade beans and mushrooms on whole wheat. While at lunchtime, look to traditional deli diner sarnies such as pastrami and giardiniera on soft brown bread or the salmon, cream cheese and caper bagel.

KEY ROASTER
Avenue Coffee Roasting Co.

BREWING METHOD
Espresso

MACHINE
La Marzocco FB70

GRINDERS
Mazzer Major, Mazzer Super Jolly

OPENING HOURS
Mon-Sun
8am-10pm

www.spitfireespresso.com   T: 07578 250105

f Spitfire Espresso   🐦 @spitfireglasgow   📷 @spitfireglasgow

№16. PAPERCUP COFFEE COMPANY - HIGH STREET

274 High Street, Glasgow, G4 0QT.

Tiny, quirky and colourful, this sister to the West End cafe exudes the same cheerfully hipster, community vibe – but with a bit of art student thrown in for good measure.

As a cafe selling its own-roasted coffee, it's naturally serious about ensuring a premium experience. You'll find the day's espresso and filter scrawled in marker pen on the custom La Marzocco, and coffee ground by EK 43 for espresso, V60 or AeroPress, as well as 17 hour cold brew and iced coffee.

Alongside the coffee, there's a good range of loose leaf teas, and the simple but super fresh menu of edibles includes poachie pots with fillings such as salmon, spinach and lemon or mushrooms and pecorino.

INSIDER'S TIP
WE LIKE THE PAPERCUP ETHOS OF 'SUPPORT LOCAL ... ALWAYS'

Whatever you do, however, DO NOT MISS the brioche french toast with smoked bacon and burnt butter – with a caramelised banana on the side. It's guaranteed to keep the Glasgow winter chill at bay.

Coffee gear is available to buy here and the team also runs latte art classes.

KEY ROASTER
Papercup Coffee Company

BREWING METHODS
Espresso, V60, AeroPress cold brew

MACHINE
La Marzocco Linea

GRINDER
Mahlkonig EK 43

OPENING HOURS
Mon-Fri 8am-4pm
Sat-Sun 10am-5pm

Gluten FREE
COFFEE BEANS AVAILABLE
ALTERNATIVE MILK
WIFI
CYCLE FRIENDLY
OUTDOOR seating
COFFEE COURSES AVAILABLE
FAMILY friendly
DISABLED ACCESS
BRING YOUR OWN Cup

www.papercupcoffee.co.uk   T: 07719 454376

f Papercup Coffee Company   🐦 @pccoffeeuk   📷 @pccoffeeuk

17. MCCUNE SMITH

3-5 Duke Street, Glasgow, G4 0UL.

The backbone of old Glasgow High Street was, for centuries, the centre of life in the city, linking its origins at the cathedral to the merchants at Glasgow Cross.

'The area at the bottom of the High Street used to be called The Coffee House Land and was where Scotland's first coffee shop was situated,' says Dan Taylor of McCune Smith.

History runs deep in this coffee enterprise, which is named after James McCune Smith, the first African American man to be awarded a medical degree.

INSIDER'S TIP THE BROTHERS SOURCE NON-HOMOGENISED MOSSGIEL MILK FROM AYRSHIRE

It all came together as a concept for Dan on a slave walk through the Merchant City area of Glasgow when he was searching for a name for the venture with his brother Simon.

The pair, who grew up in a farming community in the Hebrides wanted to create a cafe that would support Scotland's local larder and serve high quality coffee to match. And the result is a pleasingly pared back and friendly little cafe in which to mull over the rich history of coffee in Scotland, while enjoying a Dear Green pourover.

KEY ROASTER
Dear Green
Coffee Roasters

BREWING METHODS
Espresso, Kalita Wave, AeroPress

MACHINE
Royal Synchro

GRINDERS
Mazzer, Mahlkonig Tanzania

OPENING HOURS
Mon-Fri 8am-4pm
Sat 9am-5pm

www.mccunesmith.co.uk   T: 01415 481114

f McCune Smith Cafe   🐦 @mccunesmithcafe   📷 @mccunesmithcafe

MAP No. 18. TAPA ORGANIC

721 Pollokshaws Road, Strathbungo, Glasgow, G41 2AA.

Photos: Gavin Smart Photography www.viewfromtheoutside.net

It's all about the homemade at Tapa; from the coffee which the team has been roasting in Glasgow for a decade – *'we're sticking to our belief that people roast better than computers,'* is the motto of this family business – to the Soil Association certified baked goods which are hand crafted at the Tapa Organic Bakery in Dennistoun.

The bakery is where the business started and its artisan baked and certified organic bread and delicious sweet and savoury pastries form the bedrock of the edible offerings here, as at the sister cafes in Dennistoun and Kilmacolm.

INSIDER'S TIP: THE TEAM SERVES UP A CRACKING SELECTION OF VEGAN DISHES

With its neighbourhood cafe vibe, Tapa is a place to get stuck into a healthy breakfast or lunch (with vegan and gluten-free options) of homemade soup or a savoury stuffed pastry and salad, followed by good coffee.

And you can even take the beans and breads away to replicate the delicious experience at home.

KEY ROASTER
Tapa Coffee

BREWING METHODS
Espresso,
AeroPress,
french press

MACHINE
La Marzocco
Linea

GRINDER
Fiorenzato F83 E

OPENING HOURS
Mon-Sat
8am-6pm
Sun 9am-6pm

---

www.tapacoffee.com   **T:** 0141 4239494

f Tapa Organic   🐦 @tapaorganic   📷 @tapaorganic

AREA 3

SABLE & FLEA
№ 23

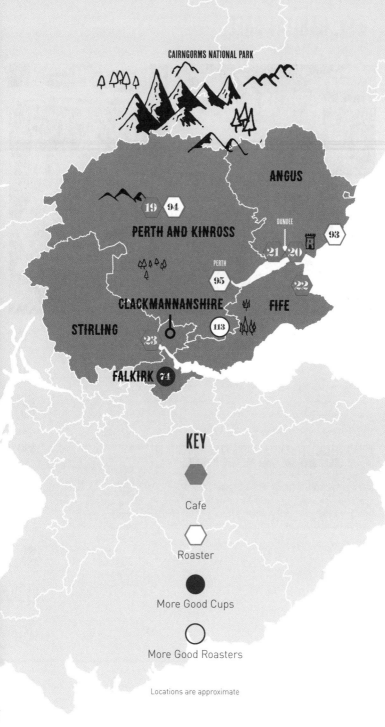

CAIRNGORMS NATIONAL PARK

ANGUS

19 94

PERTH AND KINROSS

DUNDEE

21 20 93

PERTH

95

CLACKMANNANSHIRE

FIFE

STIRLING

113

23

FALKIRK 74

KEY

Cafe

Roaster

More Good Cups

More Good Roasters

Locations are approximate

MAP 19. HABITAT CAFE

1 The Square, Aberfeldy, Perthshire, PH15 2DD.

Mike and Jan Haggerton researched every glen in Scotland before opening their cracking cafe on the corner of Aberfeldy's pretty town square. Since then they've won a glut of awards for their speciality brews, making any visit here a full-on sensory experience.

Those into bean exploration can do no better than work their way through Mike's dedicated brewing bar, which showcases everything from Woodneck to Bee House.

INSIDER'S TIP DELISH LEGENDARY BURGERS FROM TWO CUTS OF LOCAL BEEF ARE DAILY PRESSED TO ORDER

And don't worry that the adventure might lead to one coffee too many. The couple are also involved in Scotland's tea growing revolution, working closely with local farmers Dalreoch.

'We provide them with professional feedback on new tea products, such as the Isle of Mull matcha green tea and Scotland's first oolong tea, which is in progress.'

Sit at the farmhouse tables – inside or out – and enjoy a locally sourced menu and friendly vibe. Mike's Goldendoodle puppy, Hendrix, makes regular appearances, causing chaos and raising grins from customers.

KEY ROASTER
Has Bean Coffee

BREWING METHODS
Espresso, V60, AeroPress, Chemex, syphon, Clever Dripper, Kalita Wave, Woodneck, Bee House

MACHINE
Nuova Simonelli Aurelia II T3

GRINDERS
Compak, Mahlkonig

OPENING HOURS
Seasonal

 Gluten FREE

 COFFEE BEANS AVAILABLE

 ALTERNATIVE MILK

 WiFi

 CYCLE FRIENDLY

 OUTDOOR seating

 FAMILY friendly

 DISABLED ACCESS

 BRING YOUR OWN Cup

---

www.habitatcafe.co.uk   T: 01887 822944

f Habitat Cafe   🐦 @habitatcafe   📷 @habitatcafeaberfeldy

MAP №20. THE BACH

20 Exchange Court, Exchange Street, Dundee, DD1 3DE.

A bach (pronounced batch) is a Kiwi holiday home in which to escape for a long weekend, eat food cooked on the barbie and hang out with mates.

And while it's unlikely that the New Zealand owners will let you stay for the whole weekend at The Bach, you are invited to visit, get stuck into the food, imbibe a coffee or two and lose track of time with friends.

INSIDER'S TIP THE POPULAR WEEKEND BRUNCH MENU INCLUDES A LEGENDARY EGGS BENEDICT

A newcomer to Dundee, which only opened in July 2016, it's somewhere to try out a range of outstanding beans from local roaster Sacred Grounds Coffee Company.

Find the Kiwi cafe by heading for the car park in the middle of Exchange Street and look up. It's worth it for the fresh-from-the-kitchen veggie and meaty dishes. And you might just be tempted to stock up on a pocketful of Kiwi treats too; get your chops around pineapple lumps, chocolate fish, Rashuns and Twisties.

KEY ROASTER
Sacred Grounds
Coffee Company

BREWING METHODS
Espresso, V60,
AeroPress,
Chemex, syphon

MACHINE
Rocket Espresso
RES

GRINDER
Fiorenzato

OPENING HOURS
Mon-Wed
8am-9pm
Thu-Fri
8am-10pm
Sat 9am-10pm
Sun 9am-5pm

 Gluten FREE

 COFFEE BEANS AVAILABLE

 ALTERNATIVE MILK

 WIFI

 CYCLE FRIENDLY

 COFFEE COURSES AVAILABLE

 FAMILY FRIENDLY

www.the-bach.com   T: 01382 869902

f The Bach   @ @thebachbistro

MAP 21. PACAMARA FOOD AND DRINK

302 Perth Road, Dundee, DD2 1AU.

The soft background clatter of china, wafts of freshly ground coffee and plates stacked high with poached eggs and avo; forget the somewhat cooler climate of Dundee and you could be chilling in one of Melbourne's famous brunch spots at this Aussie inspired hangout.

The city's original coffee house, Espress Oh! matured into Pacamara in 2013 to create a speciality coffee shop as serious about its edible offering as its single origin brews.

INSIDER'S TIP HUNGRY? GET YOUR CHOPS AROUND ONE OF THE BADASS BURGERS

Has Bean's Jailbreak and at least two guest beans on the grinders fuel the steady crowd of caffeine hungry callers, with back up from a drool-worthy breakfast, brunch and lunch bill.

Exposed wood and chandeliers give the cafe a vintage feel: 'We always wanted to create a space that would appeal to a broad range of customers,' says owner Barry Thomson, 'and when I see the people that fill our cafe daily, I feel we got that just right.'

KEY ROASTER
Has Bean Coffee

BREWING METHODS
Espresso,
AeroPress

MACHINE
La Spaziale S9

GRINDERS
Mahlkonig K30,
Mahlkonig EK 43

OPENING HOURS
Mon-Fri 9am-5pm
Sat 9.30am-5pm
Sun 10am-4pm

 Gluten FREE

 COFFEE BEANS AVAILABLE

 ALTERNATIVE MILK

 OUTDOOR seating

 FAMILY FRIENDLY

 DISABLED ACCESS

 BRING YOUR OWN Cup

www.pacamara.co.uk   T: 01382 527666

f Pacamara Food & Drink   🐦 @pacamaradundee   📷 @pacamaradundee

№22. ZEST CAFE

95 South Street, St Andrews, Fife, KY16 9QW.

A zest for training, inclusivity and superb coffee has seen this innovative cafe, with its unique community vibe, scoop a glut of prestigious business awards.

Owner Lisa Cathro is passionate – both about her staff getting the best grounding in all things bean related (there are two SCA qualified teachers in the team), and also about the time she invests in employing and developing people with disabilities, mental health issues and those facing barriers to employment.

INSIDER'S TIP BUILD YOUR OWN FRESH FOOD PLATTER AT ZEST SALAD BAR ON MARKET STREET

But her idea of using speciality coffee as a tool for social enterprise doesn't stop there.

'We recently developed a prison barista-training programme in conjunction with hospitality charity, Springboard UK, and are looking to roll it out to other prisons after its huge success,' she says.

The friendly cafe is a great place to grab a Glen Lyon espresso with a waffle, scone or bagel. Or, on a fine day, join the horde of students, locals and visitors taking advantage of alfresco lunching under its smart awning, which happily falls on the sunny side of the street.

KEY ROASTER
Glen Lyon
Coffee Roasters

BREWING METHODS
Espresso, V60,
drip filter, cold brew

MACHINE
La Marzocco

GRINDERS
Ceado E7,
Mahlkonig K30,
Mahlkonig Vario,
Mazzer Luigi Major

OPENING HOURS
Mon-Sun
8am-6pm

 Gluten FREE

 COFFEE BEANS AVAILABLE

 ALTERNATIVE MILK

 WIFI

 CYCLE FRIENDLY

 OUTDOOR SEATING

 COFFEE COURSES AVAILABLE

 FAMILY FRIENDLY

 DISABLED ACCESS

www.wearezest.co.uk   T: 01334 471451

f Zest Café   🐦 @zeststandrews   📷 @zeststandrews

№23. SABLE & FLEA

12 Friars Street, Stirling, FK8 1HA.

Returning to Scotland after 24 years in caffeine-mad Melbourne, interior designer Suzi Carr wasn't ready to give up her quality coffee fix when she moved to speciality-sparse Stirling in 2015. With plans already in place to relocate her vintage store to the town, adding a coffee house to the proceedings was a no-brainer.

Housing an eclectic collection of Victorian furniture and designer homewares, along with a sleek coffee bar set-up, there's plenty of interior inspo to be discovered over a morning flattie at Sable & Flea.

INSIDER'S TIP BARISTA MATT'S PARENTS OFTEN SEND BEANS FROM DOWN UNDER, SO LOOK OUT FOR A TASTE OF SYDNEY IN STIRLING

A Nude Espresso house blend provides the shop's regulars with a hit of Australian cafe culture, while guest roasters offer an alternative on filter. The food from the little kitchen is healthy but hearty, with plates such as avocado and feta with balsamic and honey changing by the week. Ingredients are often organic and locally sourced, including the homemade cakes and must-try chocolate Italian buns.

KEY ROASTER
Nude Espresso

BREWING METHODS
Espresso, V60

MACHINE
La Marzocco Linea

GRINDER
Mazzer

OPENING HOURS
Tue-Sat
9.30am-5pm

Gluten FREE

ALTERNATIVE MILK

WIFI

CYCLE FRIENDLY

OUTDOOR SEATING

FAMILY FRIENDLY

DISABLED ACCESS

BRING YOUR OWN CUP

www.sableandflea.com T: 01786 475597
f Sable and Flea @ @sableflea

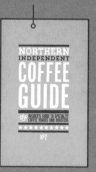

AREA 4

SÖDERBERG

№ 44

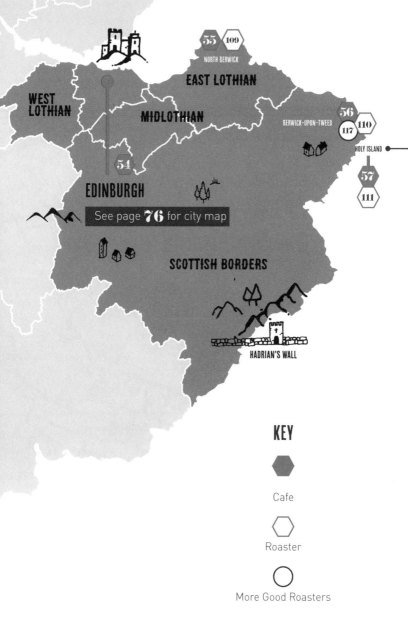

WEST LOTHIAN

EAST LOTHIAN

55 109

NORTH BERWICK

MIDLOTHIAN

56

BERWICK-UPON-TWEED

117 110

HOLY ISLAND

54

EDINBURGH

57

111

See page **76** for city map

SCOTTISH BORDERS

HADRIAN'S WALL

KEY

Cafe

Roaster

More Good Roasters

Locations are approximate

EDINBURGH CITY CENTRE

Portobello

MAP №24. RONDE BICYCLE OUTFITTERS

66-68 Hamilton Place, Stockbridge, Edinburgh, EH3 5AZ.

Cycling and coffee have long had a close relationship, and nestled in a wee corner of Stockbridge in Edinburgh, Ronde is where speciality coffee and cycling collide in the city.

The former butchers' shop retains many of its original features, although now the only carcasses hanging on the walls are those of custom-built road bikes.

Vintage ska, the hiss of the espresso steam wand and the whirr of wheels provide the soundtrack at this unique venue which specialises in bikes built to order.

INSIDER'S TIP ASK THE GUYS FOR TIPS ON THE BEST LOCAL CYCLE ROUTES

Stocking niche brands and being the home of Ronde Cycle Club, this is the racing heart of the caffeine-loving cycling community.

Go for the pre-ride pep of a double espresso or park up later for a recovery latte care of Glasgow's Avenue Coffee. And of course, you'll be needing calories: cakes are from Edinburgh's Suki-Bakes, while homemade soups and grain salads are just the ticket to fuel your ride.

KEY ROASTER
Avenue Coffee Roasting Co.

BREWING METHOD
Espresso

MACHINE
Rancilio Classe 6

GRINDER
Compak

OPENING HOURS
Mon-Wed 9am-6pm
Thu 9am-7pm
Fri-Sat 9am-6pm
Sun 11am-5pm

 Gluten FREE

 COFFEE BEANS AVAILABLE

 ALTERNATIVE MILK

 WIFI

 CYCLE FRIENDLY

 FAMILY FRIENDLY

 DISABLED ACCESS

www.rondebike.com   T: 01312 609888

f Ronde - Bicycle Outfitters   🐦 @Rondebike   📷 @rondebike

25. LEO'S BEANERY

23a Howe Street, Edinburgh, EH3 6TF.

Launching their New Town neighbourhood cafe in 2009, Joe and Marie Denby were doing the indie thing before speciality went mainstream in this pocket of the city. In the years that have passed they've added two venues – and two kids – to the family, although their thirst for great coffee has remained unchanged.

Cornish micro-roaster Hands On still supplies the house blend 80/20, with Rounton among an evolving line-up of guest roasters mixing things up.

Leo's famous brekkie menu continues to challenge those who popped in to simply sample the coffee – good luck not hunkering down and ordering a second flat white, homemade granola and poached eggs with locally smoked salmon.

INSIDER'S TIP
LEO'S NEW VENUE IS A TAPESTRY GALLERY IN VICTORIAN BATHS AT THE DOVECOT STUDIOS

With a yoga studio moving in upstairs, the cafe has upped its clean eating game to include gluten free cakes and greener goodies this year. Diet dodgers needn't panic though – the hearty winter pies and stews, doorstep sarnies and Great Taste award winning choccie brownies aren't going anywhere fast.

KEY ROASTER
Hands On

BREWING METHOD
Espresso

MACHINE
La Marzocco

GRINDER
Mazzer Super Jolly

OPENING HOURS
Mon-Fri 8am-5pm
Sat 9am-5pm
Sun 10am-5pm

www.leosbeanery.co.uk   T: 01315 568403

f Leo's Beanery   🐦 @leosbeanery   📷 @leosbeanery

BREW LAB COFFEE
№ 46

MAP №26. ARTISAN ROAST - BROUGHTON STREET

57 Broughton Street, Edinburgh, EH1 3RJ.

Artisan Roast opened in 2007 and, as a founder of Edinburgh's speciality scene, its three cafes (see More Good Cups for details of the others) should definitely be high on the lust list of any coffee lover exploring the capital.

The Broughton Street cafe is not only Artisan by name, it's also artisan in feel, with plenty of quirky paraphernalia to feast the eyes upon, against a backdrop of rustic wooden tables and floors.

Shelves groan under the weight of coffee bags and related gear in this characterful caffeine haunt, which has been featured in almost every travel magazine and newspaper article recommending Edinburgh's hipster speciality scene.

'Being coffee roasters always allows us to have a seasonal selection of up to ten different beans from around the world - the best we can get our hands on,' says owner Gustavo Pardo.

INSIDER'S TIP DURING YOUR VISIT, STOCK UP ON A WHOLE RANGE OF OWN-ROASTED GOODIES

Whichever bean you bagsy, the friendly, award winning, in-the-know baristas offer plenty of ways to brew it alongside top-notch espressos pulled through the sleek La Marzocco Linea PB.

KEY ROASTER
Artisan Roast
Coffee Roasters

BREWING METHODS
Espresso, V60,
AeroPress,
Chemex, syphon

MACHINE
La Marzocco
Linea PB

GRINDERS
Mahlkonig K30,
Mazzer Major
Electronic

OPENING HOURS
Mon-Fri 8am-7pm
Sat 10am-7pm
Sun 10am-6pm

Gluten FREE

COFFEE BEANS AVAILABLE

ALTERNATIVE MILK

OUTDOOR seating

COFFEE COURSES AVAILABLE

FAMILY FRIENDLY

BRING YOUR OWN cup

www.artisanroast.co.uk   T: 07752 078779

f Artisan Roast   🐦 @artisanroast   📷 @artisan_roast

MAP №27. FORTITUDE COFFEE

3c York Place, Edinburgh, EH1 3EB.

With rad tunes through the speakers, rustic reclaimed flooring and a choice of four rotating single origin brews on the go, Fortitude Coffee may be one of the smallest speciality bars in Edinburgh, yet it's built a huge reputation. It's known for consistent coffee, character and chatty staff.

Grab a pew by the window and watch the trams go by while you enjoy a Kalita Wave pourover or the popular in-house cold brew.

INSIDER'S TIP FOR ALL THINGS BEAN AND BREW RELATED, QUIZ THE BARISTAS WHO ARE A BUNCH OF SELF-CONFESSED COFFEE BUFFS

'Our cold brew is available all year around and is made with the help of sonic waves, which release the oaky, golden fruit flavours of our Kenyan coffee,' says owner Matt Carroll. *'It feels as special as a dram of Scottish whisky.'*

The cafe, part of the Disloyal Seven (a loyalty card scheme with six other speciality joints in the city), has recently started roasting its own coffee, which is available to buy at the counter or online.

KEY ROASTER
Fortitude Coffee Roasters

BREWING METHODS
Espresso,
Kalita Wave

MACHINE
La Marzocco
Linea PB

GRINDERS
Mahlkonig EK 43,
Victoria Arduino
Mythos One, Anfim
Super Caimano

OPENING HOURS
Mon–Fri 8am-6pm
Sat 10am-6pm
Sun 11am-4pm

 Gluten FREE

 COFFEE BEANS AVAILABLE

 ALTERNATIVE MILK

 WIFI

 BRING YOUR OWN Cup.

---

www.fortitudecoffee.com   T: 01315 573063

f Fortitude Coffee   🐦 @fortitudecoffee   📷 @fortitudecoffee

²⁸. URBAN ANGEL

121 Hanover Street, Edinburgh, EH2 1DJ.

Celebrating 11 years at Hanover Street in the city centre, the team at Urban Angel is clearly doing something right. And that thing is serving coffee that's as good as its food. Because this is not a coffee shop that does good grub, it's a restaurant that serves good coffee. And we all know how rare that is.

But coffee is taken as seriously as the cooking here, with barista Jaro Mikos ensuring that the last thing a customer tastes is as good as the first. That's why he is experimenting with beans from different roasteries including Glen Lyon, Union Hand-Roasted, Alchemy and North Star, serving it up as espresso and batch brew – with V60s on the cards.

INSIDER'S TIP WITH ITS IN-HOUSE PASTRY CHEF, THIS IS THE PLACE TO HEAD MID AFTERNOON

Venture through the building to the various quirky basement rooms in which to eat and sip coffee, where original features such as a large blackened range and bread oven provide a charming sense of history.

KEY ROASTER
Various

BREWING METHODS
Espresso,
batch brew,
cold brew

MACHINES
La Marzocco
Linea 2 group,
Bunn batch brewer

GRINDERS
Nuova Simonelli
Mythos One,
Mahlkonig Tanzania

OPENING HOURS
Mon-Fri 8am-5pm
Sat-Sun 9am-5pm

Gluten FREE · COFFEE BEANS AVAILABLE · ALTERNATIVE MILK · WIFI · CYCLE FRIENDLY · OUTDOOR SEATING · FAMILY FRIENDLY · BRING YOUR OWN CUP

www.urban-angel.co.uk   T: 01312 256215

f Urban Angel   🐦 @urbanangelcafe   📷 @urbanangel_cafe

MAP No. 29. WELLINGTON COFFEE

33a George Street, Edinburgh, EH2 2HN.

You won't find Wi-Fi, an extensive breakfast menu or a long list of serve styles at Wellington Coffee, just expertly prepared espresso and a couple of bakes on the counter – and we're down with that.

Tucked away in a wee basement on the corner of smart George and Hanover Street, this serious coffee shop provides a caffeinated refuge from Edinburgh's bustling shopping streets above.

INSIDER'S TIP — WEARY PUPS ARE ALSO WELCOME AT THIS PETIT PITSTOP

Chose between the bi-weekly guest coffee – sourced from a range of international roasters – and the Square Mile house blend, with every cup prepared with style on the Synesso machine. Each barista has learnt their trade from owner, and former Scottish Barista Champ, Jon Sharp.

Indulgent hot chocs, homemade scones and traditional shortbread are on hand for a sweet fix and make good fuel for a return to the crowds up top.

KEY ROASTER
Square Mile
Coffee Roasters

BREWING METHOD
Espresso

MACHINE
Synesso

GRINDER
Mythos

OPENING HOURS
Mon-Fri 7am-6pm
Sat 8am-6pm
Sun 9am-6pm

COFFEE BEANS AVAILABLE

ALTERNATIVE MILK

CYCLE FRIENDLY

OUTDOOR SEATING

BRING YOUR OWN CUP

T: 01312 256854

30. LOWDOWN COFFEE

40 George Street, Edinburgh, EH2 2LE.

There are loads of coffee shops in Edinburgh, but among the select few which serve speciality coffee with flair, there's a delightful variety of experiences to be had. And if you're after an individual space, focused on craft, Lowdown is your go-to.

Located in the basement of an elegant Georgian building on busy George Street, Lowdown's team uses an EKK 43 grinder for espresso; unusual as it adds considerably to the workflow, *'but we think the benefits are worth it,'* says owner Paul Anderson.

INSIDER'S TIP PICK UP RARE AND INTERESTING BEANS TO BREW AT HOME

Only seasonal, exciting and expressive beans are on offer, from roasteries such as Bath's Colonna Coffee and Koppi of Sweden; the open layout of the bar giving guests an insight into how the coffees are prepared.

If it all sounds very particular, don't be deterred, it's a sociable spot where tucking into a slice of homemade cake with a Kalita Wave is charming and cosy. And you can be safe in the knowledge that you're not wasting your caffeine allowance on anything but a safe bet.

KEY ROASTER
Colonna Coffee

BREWING METHODS
Espresso, pourover

MACHINE
Slayer V3

GRINDER
Mahlkonig EKK 43

OPENING HOURS
Mon-Fri 8am-6pm
Sat 9am-6pm
Sun 10am-6pm

 Gluten FREE

 COFFEE BEANS AVAILABLE

 ALTERNATIVE MILK

 WIFI

 CYCLE FRIENDLY

 OUTDOOR seating

 FAMILY FRIENDLY

 BRING YOUR OWN Cup

T: 01312 262132

f Lowdown Coffee 🐦 @coffeelowdown 📷 @lowdown_coffee

31. CAIRNGORM COFFEE – FREDERICK STREET

41a Frederick Street, Edinburgh, EH2 1EP.

Photos: Gavin Smart Photography www.viewfromtheoutside.net

This is the original Cairngorm and it created such an enthusiastic following that owner Robi opened a sister cafe on nearby Melville Street.

In a basement bang in the heart of the city, the Frederick Street gaff is cosy and welcoming, with enthusiastic staff who love to talk coffee with the customers – but there's so much more to it than that.

Firstly, you need to know about the grilled cheese toasties for which Cairngorm is loved. Thickly sliced bread (buttered on the outside of course), chilli jam and a bounteous volume of cheddar squished between the hot plates of a griddle, pack a crunchy, oozing punch with a calorific load to see you from breakfast to dinner.

INSIDER'S TIP IPADS ARE FITTED IN THE WALLS FOR BROWSING WHILE SIPPING

Then there's the coffee. Beans change regularly – there is no house roast – taking customers on journeys across the globe. A variety of roasters feature, including La Cabra, Good Life, Obadiah and Caravan.

KEY ROASTER
Various

BREWING METHODS
Espresso,
Kalita Wave

MACHINE
La Marzocco
Linea

GRINDER
Mahlkonig EK 43

OPENING HOURS
Mon-Fri
7.30am-6pm
Sat-Sun
9am-6pm

COFFEE BEANS AVAILABLE

ALTERNATIVE MILK

WIFI

OUTDOOR SEATING

BRING YOUR OWN CUP

---

www.cairngormcoffee.com   T: 01316 291420

f Cairngorm Coffee Co.   🐦 @cairngormcoffee   📷 @cairngormcoffeeco

MAP No 32. CASTELLO COFFEE CO.

7a Castle Street, Edinburgh, EH2 3AH.

They say good things come in small packages and that's certainly the case at Castello Coffee Co. in Edinburgh.

The miniature coffee shop is just off Princes Street, right in the centre of the city, and can probably boast the best view of the castle of any coffee shop in Edinburgh. So on sunny days the outside seating area is always busy.

INSIDER'S TIP CASTELLO STOCKS A WIDE RANGE OF MULTI COLOURED KEEPCUPS

On the coffee front, the team specialises in espresso, and its La Marzocco GB5 is kept in pristine order and buffed to perfection in honour of its important job. Allpress Espresso beans are the house choice and every single dose is weighed in and out to ensure that each serve is as good as it can possibly be.

The same care and attention is lavished on customers, with service that's very friendly and inclusive, as owner Sandro and team are keen to encourage people to support local and independent cafes and discover a better coffee experience than they get in the chains.

KEY ROASTER
Allpress Espresso

BREWING METHOD
Espresso

MACHINE
La Marzocco GB5

GRINDERS
Mazzer,
Nuova Simonelli

OPENING HOURS
Mon-Fri
7.30am-6pm
Sat 8.30am-6pm
Sun 10am-6pm

 Gluten FREE

 COFFEE BEANS AVAILABLE

 ALTERNATIVE MILK

 OUTDOOR SEATING

 DISABLED ACCESS

 BRING YOUR OWN Cup

T: 01312 259780

f Castello Coffee Co.   🐦 @castellocoffee   📷 @castellocoffee

MAP № 33. CAIRNGORM COFFEE – MELVILLE PLACE

1 Melville Place, Edinburgh, EH3 7PR.

Photos: Gavin Smart Photography, www.viewfromtheoutside.net

Fans of the original Cairngorm coffee shop on Frederick Street have been flocking to the modernist style No 2 which opened in spring 2016.

Instead of the stone and rough hewn wood of the original, you'll find sleek polished concrete and copper counter tops, gleaming white walls and huge windows overlooking the splendour of New Town. It all feels rather San Fran.

INSIDER'S TIP GO SEE SCOTLAND'S FIRST SANREMO OPERA COFFEE MACHINE!

Coffee slurpers perch at bars throughout this airy, contemporary space making it communal and friendly. Mini iPads fixed to the walls are a nod to the original Cairngorm, as are the doorstep sarnies: the famous cheese toastie is still the big hitter, with seasonally changing on-toast specials coming a close second.

Coffee is taken very seriously (in a fun kinda way) and regularly changes to showcase different styles from across the world, with guests including Caravan and Obadiah.

KEY ROASTERS
Good Life Coffee,
La Cabra
Coffee Roasters

BREWING METHODS
Espresso, Kalita
Wave, batch brew

MACHINE
Sanremo Opera
3 group

GRINDERS
Victoria Arduino
Mythos x 2,
Mahlkonig EK 43

OPENING HOURS
Mon-Fri 8am-6pm
Sat-Sun 9am-6pm

Gluten FREE

COFFEE BEANS AVAILABLE

ALTERNATIVE MILK

WIFI

OUTDOOR SEATING

BRING YOUR OWN Cup.

www.cairngormcoffee.com   T: 01316 291420

f Cairngorm Coffee Co.   🐦 @cairngormcoffee   📷 @cairngormcoffeeco

34. THE COUNTER - USHER HALL

The Police Box, Lothian Road, Edinburgh, EH1 2DJ.

It's great to see a little piece of Edinburgh's history re-purposed to good – and caffeinated – use.

Since August 2015, this old police box has been kitted out with a Sanremo Zoe Compact espresso machine and Stardust grinder so that passing shoppers and commuters can grab quality coffee to-go.

People visiting, working and appearing at Usher Hall, one of the city's most historic and grand theatres also make good use of the kiosk, and must surely appreciate the supply of excellent espresso based coffee on tap.

INSIDER'S TIP: THERE ARE PLANS AFOOT TO OPEN IN THE EVENINGS DURING THE FESTIVAL

'We are there with consistently great coffee, no matter how hard the Edinburgh wind blows,' says proprietor Sally.

The beans come courtesy of the city's Mr Eion roastery and for a little something sweet to accompany, homemade biscuits (the salted caramel cookie is especially good) and brownies are worth plumping for.

KEY ROASTER
Mr Eion
Coffee Roasters

BREWING METHOD
Espresso

MACHINE
Sanremo Zoe
Compact

GRINDER
Sanremo Stardust

OPENING HOURS
Mon-Fri
7.30am-3pm

COFFEE BEANS AVAILABLE

ALTERNATIVE MILK

CYCLE FRIENDLY

FAMILY FRIENDLY

DISABLED ACCESS

f The Counter   🐦 @thecountered   📷 @thecountered

№ 35. LOVECRUMBS

155 West Port, Edinburgh, EH3 9DP.

The sign on the blackboard at lovecrumbs states, 'Cake and tea = happy', but if you're more into coffee, you won't be disappointed. With North Berwick's Steampunk as the house roast and Glasgow's Papercup as guest, Hollie and the team are keeping things high quality and local.

And as for the cake, well, there are usually over ten different varieties on offer in the vintage sideboard, from gingerbread bundt to pear and cardamom tart with chocolate crumble. It's what the cafe is known for, but recent changes mean that savouries are increasingly sneaking onto the menu and faves such as crushed garlic peas and seeds, or grilled courgette and ricotta on sourdough, are available all day.

INSIDER'S TIP
LOVECRUMBS IS ONE OF THE FEW CAFES SERVING NITRO IN THE SUMMER

With its pleasing jumble of upcycled furniture in the space, which opened in 1845 as a grocery, there's a community vibe here. A knitting group meets every week, there's a large round table which is the perfect spot for your own tea party, and with plenty of room it's also the haunt of laptop warriors fuelled by quality caffeine.

KEY ROASTER
Steampunk Coffee

BREWING METHODS
Espresso, nitro

MACHINE
La Marzocco Linea

GRINDER
Anfim

OPENING HOURS
Mon-Fri 9am-6pm
Sat 9.30am-6pm
Sun 12pm-6pm

 Gluten FREE

 COFFEE BEANS AVAILABLE

 ALTERNATIVE MILK

 WIFI

 CYCLE FRIENDLY

 BRING YOUR OWN Cup

---

www.lovecrumbs.co.uk   T: 01316 290626

f Lovecrumbs   🐦 @hellolovecrumbs   📷 @hellolovecrumbs

MAP N°36. MACHINA ESPRESSO - TOLLCROSS

2 Brougham Place, Tollcross, Edinburgh, EH3 9HW.

The original Machina coffee bar and store, this is one of the few places in the city where you can lay your hands on everything from a syphon or filter to high end grinders – not to mention obscure spare parts for your existing kit – and get a good coffee at the same time.

The vibe is restrained: white walls, architectural wooden tables and bar, plus images of cold water surf locations, create a light, contemplative feel. A refit earlier in the year makes more of the cafe area, which seems to have been a good move. And you can also pick up high-end beans-to-go from roasteries such as Koppi, Fjord and Horsham.

INSIDER'S TIP CUP ENVY? PICK FROM THE RAINBOW ARRAY OF INKER CUPS STOCKED AT THE CAFE

While the team is very serious about coffee, simplicity shines through, and bespoke single origins roasted by Steve, Mark and Emiliya in Machina's Edinburgh roastery result in an in-house coffee to be paired with milk and one to drink black. Accompanying food is equally simple: pastries, bagels, sarnies and soup.

KEY ROASTER
Machina Espresso

BREWING METHODS
Espresso, V60, Chemex

MACHINE
La Marzocco
Linea AV 2 group

GRINDERS
Mythos One x 2

OPENING HOURS
Mon-Fri 8am-6pm
Sat 9am-6pm
Sun 10am-6pm

Gluten FREE

COFFEE BEANS AVAILABLE

ALTERNATIVE MILK

WIFI

OUTDOOR seating

COFFEE COURSES AVAILABLE

BRING YOUR OWN Cup.

www.machina-espresso.co.uk   T: 01312 293495

f Machina Espresso   🐦 @machinaespresso   📷 @machinaespresso

MAP N° 37. LEO AND TED

36 Leven Street, Edinburgh, EH3 9LJ.

In the vibrant quarter of Tollcross, Leo and Ted is a cosy sanctuary from the bustle of the outside world. Maybe it's the thick old walls which are exposed at the windows or maybe it's the calm vibe of this gently urban little coffee shop.

Slabs of toasted homemade coconut bread, or scones slathered in butter, with Leo's own 80/20 blend from Hands On has traditionally been the way to start the day here, but a new brekkie menu is changing all that.

'The best bagels you will ever eat,' according to Joe, come courtesy of The Bearded Baker and are served with eggs (benedict, florentine or royale); or go for granola or porridge. At lunch there's fresh homemade soup and stew on every day, and lots of sweet treats for tea. What you may not expect is the range of gluten free options here, which like everything else is homemade.

INSIDER'S TIP THE LEO AND TED LAND ROVER COFFEE VAN IS REVVING UP TO LAUNCH SOON

Soon you'll be able to stay on later for a thrilling range of caffeinated cocktails (plus beer and wine) when the alcohol menu kicks in. Find sister cafes Leo's Beanery and Leo's at Dovecot Studios in the city too.

KEY ROASTER
Hands On Coffee

BREWING METHODS
Espresso,
cold brew

MACHINE
La Marzocco

GRINDERS
Mazzer Super Jolly,
Mythos One

OPENING HOURS
Mon-Fri 8am-5pm
Sat 9am-5pm
Sun 10am-5pm

Gluten FREE

COFFEE BEANS AVAILABLE

ALTERNATIVE MILK

WIFI

FAMILY FRIENDLY

BRING YOUR OWN CUP

T: 01314 660400

f Leo and Ted   🐦 @leoandted   📷 @leoandted

№38. THE COUNTER ON THE CANAL

Edinburgh Basin, near Lower Gilmore Place, Edinburgh.

The newest member of the Counter clan, The Counter on the Canal was launched in spring 2016. Owners Sally and Ali McFarlane have continued their knack for converting small and unusual spaces into top quality coffee kiosks, this time renovating an old narrow boat on Union Canal near Lower Gilmore Place to become the city's only floating coffee offering.

'We're still on a learning curve – simple things become complicated when you're operating on water,' says Ali. *'We never thought we'd be pumping out bilges when we started our journey.'*

INSIDER'S TIP THE PERFECT EXCUSE FOR A WEEKEND CYCLE TRIP ALONG THE CANAL

The pair report that the coffee is helping people discover a new area of the city, and Sally says, *'we didn't know there was a canal in Edinburgh until we bought the boat'.*

As with the other Counters, the coffee is roasted to a special recipe by local roaster Mr Eion, served as beautiful espresso-based drinks and accompanied by a small but high quality selection of homemade biscuits and brownies.

KEY ROASTER
Mr Eion
Coffee Roaster

BREWING METHOD
Espresso

MACHINE
Sanremo Zoe

GRINDER
Sanremo Stardust

OPENING HOURS
Mon-Fri
7.30am-4.30pm
Sat-Sun
10am-4.30pm

 COFFEE BEANS AVAILABLE

 ALTERNATIVE MILK

 CYCLE FRIENDLY

 OUTDOOR SEATING

 FAMILY FRIENDLY

 DISABLED ACCESS

f The Counter   🐦 @thecountered   📷 @thecountered

39. PROJECT COFFEE

192-194 Bruntsfield Place, Edinburgh, EH10 4DF.

Laid-back brunching and seriously good coffee is the order of the day at Project Coffee on buzzy Bruntsfield Place.

One of six speciality shops in the city owned by former Scottish Barista Champ Jon Sharp, each cafe has a unique personality, inspired by the buildings, communities and customers that pack out the popular venues.

INSIDER'S TIP SWING BY IN THE AFTERNOON FOR PROJECT'S LEGENDARY SCONES

With tiled walls, industrial lighting and a scatter of sinkable sofas, Project's Instagramable interiors and easy-going vibe are indicative of this burgeoning indie neighbourhood. A steady stream of students, creatives and families pack out the petit venue, though tables turn quickly and a little patience is worth it for the famed brekkie offering.

Pair eggs benedict, seasonal soups or a slab of something sweet with one of the espresso based brews from the board, each carefully crafted by the clued-up baristas, using beans from London's Square Mile.

KEY ROASTER
Square Mile
Coffee Roasters

BREWING METHOD
Espresso

MACHINE
Synesso

GRINDER
Mythos

OPENING HOURS
Mon-Fri
7.30am-7pm
Sat-Sun 8am-6pm

T: 01312 296758

MAP.Nº 40. BLACKWOOD COFFEE

235 Morningside Road, Edinburgh, EH10 4QT.

Those growing weary of concrete bars, canvas cushions and more succulents than your grandma's sunroom will delight in the classic cafe charm of Morningside's Blackwood Coffee.

Sharing a street with boutique shops and grand buildings, the panelled walls and brass-topped counter and tables give this serious coffee shop a refined feel to rival any urban cool neighbours.

The calibre of the coffee is just as high, with Square Mile providing the material for the skilled baristas to master, all of whom are trained by owner, and former Scottish Barista Champion, Jon Sharp.

INSIDER'S TIP ROCK UP EARLY TO AVOID THE QUEUES AND FUEL UP ON POACHED EGGS AND BACON

Scones are big business at the bustling community hub. Pick a fruit studded lovely with proper clotted cream and rich, plummy jam, or at lunchtime swap one of the handmade sandwiches for a cheesy scone with lashings of butter. Handmade cakes and traybakes also feature, with options for gluten-dodgers too.

KEY ROASTER
Square Mile
Coffee Roasters

BREWING METHOD
Espresso

MACHINE
Synesso

GRINDER
Mythos

OPENING HOURS
Mon-Fri 8am-6pm
Sat 9am-6pm
Sun 9am-5pm

COFFEE BEANS AVAILABLE

ALTERNATIVE MILK

CYCLE FRIENDLY

OUTDOOR SEATING

FAMILY FRIENDLY

DISABLED ACCESS

BRING YOUR OWN CUP

T: 01314 460429

Nº 41. THE MILKMAN

7 Cockburn Street, Edinburgh, EH1 1BP.

Edinburgh's most charming coffee house was named after owner Mark's great grandfather – the last milkman to deliver milk by horse and cart in northern Scotland.

Historic links continue via the cafe's location in Edinburgh's magical Old Town, where its art deco – and Scottish World Heritage protected – sign welcomes visitors with a nod to its food and drink heritage. Step inside, and stripped back ancient stone walls continue to reveal the earliest cornerstones of the shop's original design.

For such a tiny nook, every inch has been thoughtfully used to harmonise history and modern need, creating spots to kick back and watch the world go by, or from which to appreciate the skills of the well-trained and friendly baristas on the espresso machine.

INSIDER'S TIP
THE VINTAGE-STYLE MILKSHAKES LOOK TO BECOME A HOUSE SPECIALITY

Glasgow's Dear Green crafts the Goosedubs house blend, while roasteries on rotation – particularly on batch brew – include Alchemy and Obadiah, for which the new EK 43 grinder does the honours.

KEY ROASTER
Dear Green
Coffee Roasters

BREWING METHODS
Espresso,
batch brew,
AeroPress

MACHINE
La Marzocco
Linea Classic

GRINDERS
Mazzer Super Jolly,
Mahlkonig EK 43

OPENING HOURS
Mon-Fri 8am-6pm
Sat-Sun 9am-6pm

 Gluten FREE

 COFFEE BEANS AVAILABLE

 ALTERNATIVE MILK

 WIFI

 DISABLED ACCESS

 BRING YOUR OWN Cup

www.themilkman.coffee   T: 01312 257119

f The Milkman   🐦 @themilkmanedin   📷 @themilkmancoffee

42. HULA JUICE BAR

103-105 West Bow, Edinburgh, EH1 2JP.

This buzzy, healthy hideaway in a lovely old building on curved West Bow, off the Royal Mile, is a find for its vibrant menu of juices, rainbow bowls and sandwiches.

With a rebrand and refreshed look for its tenth birthday, including a large jungle wall mural, cutlery in ceramic coconuts and verdant green furniture, this is the healthy-eating coffee lovers' happy place.

INSIDER'S TIP HULA OFFERS A HUGE SELECTION OF GLUTEN FREE, VEGAN AND RAW OPTIONS

Lots of staff mean that while it's often busy, service is quick and efficient with acai bowls or smashed beetroot on toast with aubergine jam, fried shallots and lime, delivered to your table in a jiffy.

Another new all-day fave is the maca nana bowl which is a blend of maca, vanilla and banana with almond milk, raspberry granola, blueberries and peanut butter.

On the coffee front, it's all espresso based and overseen by owner and founder Susan who is as serious about her exceptional matcha almond latte as she is the Artisan Roast coffees.

KEY ROASTER
Artisan Roast
Coffee Roasters

BREWING METHOD
Espresso

MACHINE
La Spaziale

GRINDER
Mazzer Major

OPENING HOURS
Mon-Sun
8am-6pm

www.hulajuicebar.co.uk   T: 01312 201121

f Hula Juice Bar   🐦 @hulajuicebar   📷 @hulajuicebar

43. THOMAS J WALLS

35 Forest Road, Edinburgh, EH1 2QT.

When we published last year's guide, this cafe was just a would-be rosetta in a barista's eye.

One year on, it has matured into a thoroughly charming coffee shop that's a very special find in Edinburgh.

Huge picture windows with antique gold lettering, a cosy fireplace with 1930s tiles, gleaming, original dark wood panelling and marble topped tables create charismatic elegance, while the coffee and food are equally alluring.

You won't find lots of serve styles here, but you will find a perfectly poured flat white or cappuccino that's the epitome of understated excellence. Pair it with quality cafe food – the very generous breakfasts include a cracking smoked salmon and scrambled eggs, or avocado, poached eggs and feta on sourdough.

INSIDER'S TIP
THE ROARING FIRE IS HUGELY INVITING ON A WINTRY AFTERNOON IN THE CITY

With lots of space – the ex-opticians shop goes back quite some way – you're certain to find a quiet retreat in which to indulge in a moment that feels like it's from a more glamorous age.

KEY ROASTER
Square Mile
Coffee Roasters

BREWING METHOD
Espresso

MACHINE
Synesso

GRINDER
Mythos

OPENING HOURS
Mon-Fri
7.30am-7pm
Sat-Sun
8am-7pm

COFFEE BEANS AVAILABLE

ALTERNATIVE MILK

FAMILY FRIENDLY

DISABLED ACCESS

BRING YOUR OWN CUP

T: 01312 617582

MAP Nº 44. SÖDERBERG

1 Lister Square, Edinburgh, EH3 9GL.

Get your fix of Scandi fika, decor and all-round good vibes at the burgeoning collection of Söderbergs in the city.

The Lister Square cafe is the spot for artisan bread, sourdough pizzas and pastries (oh, those cinnamon buns ...), baked fresh each day at its Quartermile bakery upstairs, along with coffee from Stockholm roaster Johan & Nyström.

INSIDER'S TIP PREPARE TO LEAVE WITH BAGS BULGING WITH A FRESHLY-BAKED CARBY HAUL

The focal point here, in the middle of all this airy, industrial-chic is the large bread oven used to cook the show-stopping pizzas. So grab a coffee, dig into that open sandwich and watch the team at work as they bring a voguish slice of Stockholm to Scotland.

If the place is packed out, Lister Street's sister venues on Simpson Loan and in Stockbridge are worth a visit, as are the new bakery shops on Broughton and Queensferry Streets.

KEY ROASTER
Johan & Nyström

BREWING METHOD
Espresso

MACHINE
La Marzocco

GRINDER
La Marzocco

OPENING HOURS
Mon 8am-5pm
Tue-Fri 8am-10.30pm
Sat 10am-10.30pm
Sun 10am-5pm

 Gluten FREE

 COFFEE BEANS AVAILABLE

 ALTERNATIVE MILK

 OUTDOOR SEATING

 FAMILY FRIENDLY

 DISABLED ACCESS

www.soderberg.uk   T: 01312 281905

f Söderberg   @ @soderbergbakery

⁴⁵45. COBOLT COFFEE

Police Box, Marchmont Crescent, Edinburgh, EH9 1HL.

Delivering top-notch coffee from a space no bigger than your typical Portaloo, Adam Glen's former police box is just one of about 70 left in Edinburgh. Cobolt is No 35 and you can ask to see the original number stamped inside.

'I'm creating neighbourhood vibes while slingin' baller spros from the roadside,' says Adam. *'And serving the community from the street means we're as accessible as it comes.'*

Cobolt is also unusual in that there's no single key roastery providing the workhorse coffee. Adam says: *'We've changed up the whole house and guest regime to focus on bringing in as many top roasts from across Scotland as possible, so now we typically use a couple of roasters over the course of a month.'*

INSIDER'S TIP: **VISIT TO APPRECIATE THE ZEN-LIKE MASTERY OF COFFEE MAKING IN THIS TINY SPACE**

It's certainly gained him a loyal band of customers in the Marchmont area which is blossoming with students, young families and working professionals, *'It's a good mix,'* smiles Adam.

KEY ROASTER
Various

BREWING METHODS
Espresso, V60, AeroPress

MACHINE
Sanremo Capri

GRINDERS
Mazzer Robur, Baratza Forté

OPENING HOURS
Mon-Fri 8am-3pm
Sat 9.30am-4pm
Extended in summer

COFFEE BEANS AVAILABLE

ALTERNATIVE MILK

CYCLE FRIENDLY

OUTDOOR SEATING

DISABLED ACCESS

T: 07772 357855

f Cobolt Coffee 🐦 @coboltcoffee 📷 @coboltcoffee

46. BREW LAB COFFEE

6-8 South College Street, Edinburgh, EH8 9AA.

A coffee tour of the capital wouldn't be complete without indulging in all things nerdy at Brew Lab in the Old Town.

Caffeine fiends flock to this slick coffee emporium for the nitro: a cold brew concoction infused with nitrogen gas to create a wickedly creamy and incredibly smooth mouthfeel. Regulars return for the comprehensive collection of coffees from guest roasters such as The Barn and La Cabra, expertly crafted by the talented team of baristas, headed up by UKBC 2016 runner-up Claire Wallace.

Brunch and lunch options match the calibre of the coffee, with a pleasing selection of seasonal salads, artisan baguettes and gorgeous baked goods. Coffee cocktails and craft beers have been added to the menu this year, as well as extended opening hours, for those looking for a fix after six.

INSIDER'S TIP
GRAB A BOTTLE OF BREW LAB'S OWN COLD BREW AT SPECIALITY SHOPS ACROSS SCOTLAND

In the basement you'll find the Brew training lab, where the caffeine curious come to learn the tricks of the trade. Masterclasses include espresso, filter and sensory classes, as well as bespoke lessons and barista training.

KEY ROASTER
Has Bean Coffee

BREWING METHODS
Espresso,
Kalita Wave,
cold brew

MACHINE
Victoria Arduino
VA388 Black Eagle
Gravimetric

GRINDER
Nuova Simonelli
Mythos One

OPENING HOURS
Mon-Fri 8am-6pm
Sat-Sun 9am-6pm

 Gluten FREE

 COFFEE BEANS AVAILABLE

 ALTERNATIVE MILK

 WIFI

 CYCLE FRIENDLY

 OUTDOOR SEATING

 COFFEE COURSES AVAILABLE

 FAMILY FRIENDLY

 DISABLED ACCESS

BRING YOUR OWN CUP

www.brewlabcoffee.co.uk   T: 01316 628963

f Brew Lab Coffee   🐦 @brewlabcoffee   📷 @brewlabcoffee

47. MACHINA ESPRESSO - NEWINGTON

80 Nicolson Street, Edinburgh, EH8 9EW.

Keeping up with the perpetually peckish demands of Newington's bustling student population, the second outpost of Machina is your go-to for a foodie refuel.

On offer alongside the locally made grub is espresso and batch brew that's roasted in-house by Machina, as well as guests from the highly esteemed Colonna in Bath and Fjord in Berlin. Trading beans with the German roastery, the team runs an innovative coffee swap to avoid chaotic Euro exchange rates.

Stop for coffee in this airy space with its slightly architectural feel and take it as espresso, filter or batch brew.

INSIDER'S TIP CHOOSE FROM OWN-ROASTED BEANS OR TAKE A LITTLE TRIP AROUND THE GLOBE

The coffee's paired with a stepped up menu that includes doorstep toasties, unmissable banana loaf and blueberry and pecan brownies.

KEY ROASTER
Machina Espresso

BREWING METHODS
Espresso, filter, batch brew

MACHINE
La Marzocco Linea PB

GRINDERS
Mythos One x 2

OPENING HOURS
Mon-Wed 8am-6pm
Thu-Sat 8am-7pm
Sun 9am-6pm

Gluten FREE · COFFEE BEANS AVAILABLE · ALTERNATIVE MILK · WIFI · OUTDOOR seating · COFFEE COURSES AVAILABLE · DISABLED ACCESS · BRING YOUR OWN CUP

www.machina-espresso.co.uk   T: 01316 299825

f Machina Espresso   @machinaespresso   @machinaespresso

48. KILIMANJARO COFFEE

104 Nicolson Street, Edinburgh, EH8 9EJ.

Floor to ceiling windows, a cluster of tables outside and a top spot on Edinburgh's busy Nicolson Street makes Kilimanjaro Coffee a people watching paradise.

Adopting a laid-back and informal vibe at the first of Edinburgh coffee guru Jon Sharp's coffee shops – you'll find five more tucked away in the city's nooks and crannies – is easy. It's picking just one of the jewelled bakes that embellish the counter that's the tricky part.

INSIDER'S TIP LOOK OUT FOR GUEST ROASTERS ON THE HOPPER FROM THE LIKES OF THE BARN

Pull up a pew from the collection of mismatched chairs or sink into the well-loved Chesterfield while indulging in a speciality high, courtesy of Square Mile, from the espresso based board.

Brunch is a big deal at this popular hangout – try the courgette fritters with avocado, feta, bacon, poached eggs and beetroot chutney. Though the chunky ciabatta and steaming bowls of homemade soup are also worthy of a shout out.

KEY ROASTER
Square Mile
Coffee Roasters

BREWING METHOD
Espresso

MACHINE
Synesso

GRINDER
Mythos

OPENING HOURS
Mon-Fri
7.30am-8.30pm
Sat-Sun 8am-8pm

COFFEE BEANS AVAILABLE

ALTERNATIVE MILK

CYCLE FRIENDLY

OUTDOOR SEATING

DISABLED ACCESS

BRING YOUR OWN CUP

T: 01316 620135

MAP Nº 49. PRESS COFFEE

30 Buccleuch Street, Edinburgh, EH8 9LP.

You don't have to study philosophy, or freelance at one of Edinburgh's indies, to hang out at Press Coffee on the edge of the University's campus. Though, during term time, be prepared to join the throng of students and creatives that congregate for great coffee at this popular meeting place.

When school's out, this light and airy coffee shop from Jon Sharp's band of brew houses transforms into an oasis of calm. Pack a book, pull up a chair and luxuriate in an expertly prepared coffee from Square Mile or the seasonal guest roast stocking the grinder.

INSIDER'S TIP CHECK OUT THE LOCAL ARTWORK LINING THE VIBRANT YELLOW WALLS

Freshly squeezed orange and cold pressed juices provide refreshing relief when the coffee jitters hit, with a good selection of egg-based brunch dishes and filled ciabattas also on hand. If you're after grub to-go, soup and sarnies are available to take out, along with the coffee.

KEY ROASTER
Square Mile
Coffee Roasters

BREWING METHOD
Espresso

MACHINE
Synesso

GRINDER
Mythos

OPENING HOURS
Mon-Fri 8am-6pm
Sat-Sun 9am-5pm

ALTERNATIVE MILK

CYCLE FRIENDLY

OUTDOOR SEATING

BRING YOUR OWN Cup.

T: 01316 676205

STEAMPUNK COFFEE
№ 55

MAP №50. FILAMENT COFFEE

38 Clerk Street, Edinburgh, EH8 9HX.

It may have had a bit of a spruce up inside and the addition of some rather cool artwork across the walls since last year's guide, but Filament's serious-about-speciality vibe and quality of cup is the same as ever.

The Mythos One and EK 43 grinders earn their crust hourly, whizzing up single origin beans from across the globe. These are roasted by the likes of Staffordshire's Has Bean for the house roast with London's Square Mile and Edinburgh's Williams and Johnson on guest.

INSIDER'S TIP GET STUCK INTO A CONSTANTLY ROTATING MENU OF SINGLE ORIGINS

Drop by for a coffee to-go or grab a pew and choose from the über simplified menu of black, white or filter (the detail being in the beans rather than the variety of serves) and chill out for a while with a Bearded Baker bagel and excellent tunes for company.

KEY ROASTER
Has Bean Coffee

BREWING METHODS
Espresso,
AeroPress

MACHINE
Nuova Simonelli
Aurelia

GRINDERS
Mythos One,
Mahlkonig EK 43

OPENING HOURS
Mon-Fri
7.30am-7pm
Sat 9am-6pm
Sun 9am-5pm

COFFEE BEANS AVAILABLE

ALTERNATIVE MILK

WIFI

DISABLED ACCESS

BRING YOUR OWN cup.

51. CULT ESPRESSO
104 Buccleuch Street, Edinburgh, EH8 9NQ.

Photos: Gavin Smart Photography www.viewfromtheoutside.net

It's easy to pass by Cult Espresso and assume that it's nothing more than a tiny hole in the wall. Step inside though and you'll instantly get the TARDIS effect, as the cavernous space stretches way back.

So grab yourself one of the comfy spots and hide away for the afternoon with a Kalita Wave brew, avo toast and Lego – yep Lego. There's quite a collection of *Star Wars* characters who've taken up residence here.

Garry Stone's conversion to the coffee world started with a small kiosk at Dalmeny Railway Station before he decided to let his hobby run away with him. Now, alongside dad Kevin, brother Jason and friend Drew, their industrial loft-style cafe has become a friendly neighbourhood coffee destination.

INSIDER'S TIP THE GUYS SOMETIMES EXCHANGE COFFEE FOR LEGO - TRY YOUR LUCK

Serving only single origin coffees (*'we believe this is the best way to bring out the coffees' best flavours'*) from Round Hill Roastery and a regularly changing rota of guest European roasters, means there's something exciting to guzzle alongside every satisfying soup, sandwich or bake.

KEY ROASTER
Round Hill Roastery

BREWING METHODS
Espresso, Kalita Wave, AeroPress

MACHINE
Kees Van Der Westen Mirage

GRINDERS
Mahlkonig K30, Mythos One

OPENING HOURS
Mon-Fri 8am-6pm
Sat 10am-6pm
Sun 10am-5pm

Gluten FREE

COFFEE BEANS AVAILABLE

ALTERNATIVE MILK

WIFI

CYCLE FRIENDLY

OUTDOOR SEATING

---

www.cult-espresso.com   T: 01316 628083

f Cult Espresso   🐦 @cultcoffeeedin   📷 @cult_espresso

ᴺᵒ52. CENTURY GENERAL STORE AND CAFE

1-7 Montrose Terrace, Edinburgh, EH7 5DJ.

So what is a tomahawk? It's the question that Niall, barista and part owner of Century gets asked on a daily basis. It's basically a cortado (or piccolo, or flat white with less milk) that a regular customer (Tom) described as his ideal coffee. And so the tomahawk - served in a handmade ceramic cup – was born.

Designing things is a big deal round here; half the store sells 'timeless essentials for everyday joy', while the other half is an airy cafe. Long-time Edinburgh coffee specialist Niall is the bean freak, Stevey curates the homewares.

INSIDER'S TIP THE PERFECT STOP ON YOUR WAY DOWN FROM ARTHUR'S SEAT

Niall has chosen London's Assembly Coffee as the house roast, alongside a regularly rotating group of guests such as local roasters Williams and Johnson, and Oslo's Tim Wendelboe.

Launching in January 2016, with its collection of artisan crafts and unusual publications, it's rather like being at the home of an extremely stylish friend – who's also a whizz on the La Marzocco. Damn them.

KEY ROASTER
Assembly Coffee

BREWING METHOD
Espresso

MACHINE
La Marzocco
Linea Classic

GRINDERS
Mazzer Robur E,
Anfim x 2

OPENING HOURS
Tue-Fri 8am-5pm
Sat 9am-5pm
Sun 10am-5pm

www.centurygeneralstore.com

f Century General Store   🐦 @centurygeneral   📷 @centurygeneralstore

53. BABA BUDAN

Arch 13, East Market Street, Edinburgh, EH8 8FS.

This new cafe and donutterie underneath the arches near the Royal Mile is converting Scots from shortbread to doughnuts, one crisp, doughy ball of delight at a time.

With its bakery next door turning out a smörgåsbord of flavoured doughnuts each day – we especially like the salted chocolate, BTW – and quality coffee from the likes of The Coffee Collective and Square Mile, it won't be long until the customers are queuing all the way from Princes Street.

'We've spent time deciding on and getting to know the coffee we use and finding out what our customers like,' says owner Craig. *'We pride ourselves on serving a coffee we love, a beautiful espresso from Coffee Collective, which you currently can't get anywhere else in the city.'*

Choose an espresso based or batch brew filter coffee and pair it with a savoury bagel if you can't take the sugar/caffeine buzz.

INSIDER'S TIP TAKE THE SUGAR FIX FURTHER WITH HANDMADE CHOCS MADE IN THEIR KITCHEN NEXT DOOR

Canines are as well looked after as their human chums, with doggie treats and biscuits available, plus there's outdoor seating. Look out for acoustic sets on Sundays and an upcoming diary of musical events.

KEY ROASTER
The Coffee Collective

BREWING METHODS
Espresso, batch brew

MACHINE
La Marzocco Linea PB

GRINDERS
Mahlkonig EK 43, Mythos One

OPENING HOURS
Mon-Fri
7.30am-5pm
Sat-Sun
9.30am-5pm

www.bababudan.coffee   T: 07753 742550

f Baba Budan   🐦 @bababudancoffee   📷 @bababudancoffee

MAP NO 54. NO 1 PEEBLES ROAD

1 Peebles Road, Innerleithen, EH44 6QX.

Whether you're fresh from a cycling sesh in the hills, on the trail of speciality brew in the Scottish borders or simply after a good cuppa and a chinwag with the locals, No 1 Peebles Road is keeping the sleepy village of Innerleithen's visitors well and truly wired.

With some of the country's best mountain biking routes on its doorstep, there's a constant cache of keen cyclists in search of a quick caffeine hit. Don't be deterred if the place is packed, the 25 seats turn over swiftly and with two big old farmhouse tables stretching out along the coffee shop, morning brew is a social affair. Grab a pew and start talking tasting notes on the latest Steampunk beans with your neighbour.

INSIDER'S TIP TRY THE NO 1 SURPRISE: BANANA, BACON AND MARMALADE IN ONE SANDWICH. DARE YA!

Fresh homemade fodder – think french toast with maple and bacon, avocado bruschetta and chunky sarnies – is on hand for eager appetites, with scones, cakes and traybakes for those in favour of sweet thrills.

KEY ROASTER
Steampunk Coffee

BREWING METHODS
Espresso, drip, french press

MACHINE
La Marzocco

GRINDER
Mahlkonig K30

OPENING HOURS
Thu-Tue 8am-6pm

 Gluten FREE

 COFFEE BEANS AVAILABLE

 ALTERNATIVE MILK

 WIFI

 CYCLE FRIENDLY

OUTDOOR seating

 BRING YOUR OWN cup

www.no1peeblesroad.coffee   T: 01896 830873

f No1 Peebles Road

MAP № 55. STEAMPUNK COFFEE

49a Kirk Ports, North Berwick, East Lothian, EH39 4HL.

A funky old steel-framed warehouse in the charming seaside town of North Berwick provides Steampunk Coffee with its industrial-style HQ. Originally built as a joinery workshop, owner Catherine Franks has given it a new lease of life as a vibrant coffee roastery and cafe.

Downstairs, you might like to grab a single origin espresso-based coffee and watch head roaster Dori Czegledi and her team at work on the vintage Probat roaster, squeezing the best out of every ethically sourced bean.

INSIDER'S TIP MEET MAVIS, STEAMPUNK COFFEE'S VW AT STOCKBRIDGE MARKET EVERY SUNDAY

Upstairs, you can nestle in a comfy armchair with a good book in front of one of the cosy log burners and enjoy a menu bursting with freshness. Think sandwiches oozing with golden grilled cheese or warming soups and stews. But be sure to leave room for American-style indulgences like the chewy chocolate chip cookies and addictive brownies.

KEY ROASTER
Steampunk Coffee

BREWING METHODS
Espresso, Bunn batch brewer

MACHINE
La Marzocca Linea Classic

GRINDER
Mythos One

OPENING HOURS
Mon-Sat 9am-5pm
Sun 10am-5pm

Gluten FREE

COFFEE BEANS AVAILABLE

ALTERNATIVE MILK

WIFI

CYCLE FRIENDLY

OUTDOOR SEATING

DISABLED ACCESS

BRING YOUR OWN Cup

www.steampunkcoffee.co.uk   T: 01620 893030

f Steampunk Coffee   🐦 @steampunkcoffee   📷 @steampunkcoffee

56. RIALTO COFFEE CO.

33 High Street, Eyemouth, Berwickshire, TD14 5EY.

Forget matching wine with cheese or beer with chocolate, there's a new foodie trend in town now that the guys at Rialto Coffee Co. are pairing coffee with pastries and homemade bakes.

With Avenue Coffee supplying a seasonal single origin house espresso, a guest roast in the hopper AND a not-so-secret stash of beans under the bar, there's plenty for the knowledgeable baristas to choose from.

Whatever you plump for, whether it's a savoury spanakopita (filo stuffed with feta, spinach and fresh herbs) or the two-fingers-to-the-diet dulce de leche, it will have been made from scratch in the busy kitchen of this family-run cafe.

INSIDER'S TIP: WARM UP BY THE ROARING COAL FIRE AFTER A STOMP ALONG THE BERWICKSHIRE COASTAL PATH

In addition to the small selection of coffee kit for the burgeoning home brewer, owners Michael and Eilyn Howes-Quintero have introduced pre-booked coffee courses every Saturday afternoon for customers wanting to get the most out of their new gear and beans picked up at the shop.

KEY ROASTER
Avenue Coffee
Roasting Co.

BREWING METHODS
Espresso,
Chemex

MACHINE
La Marzocco
Linea PB

GRINDER
Mahlkonig EKK 43
twin

OPENING HOURS
Tue-Sat 9am-4pm
Extended in
summer

Gluten FREE
COFFEE BEANS AVAILABLE
ALTE RNA TIVE MILK
WIFI
CYCLE FRIENDLY
COFFEE COURSES AVAILABLE
FAMILY FRIENDLY
DISABLED ACCESS

www.rialto-coffee.uk   T: 01890 752048

f Rialto Coffee Co.   🐦 @rialtocoffeeco

CONNECT

ROAST

DEVELOP

CUP

Roaster Guild of Europe is a trade guild representing the professional roasting community. Created especially for roasters, RGE wants to build a space for the European roasting community to grow and connect. Education is at the heart of this Guild and will be a key element at Roaster Camp where RGE will provide a creative, informative and progressive environment for Roasters to share and learn.

www.roasterguildofeurope.com / @roasterguild_eu / #RoasterCampEU

MAP 57. PILGRIMS COFFEE HOUSE

Falkland House, Marygate, Holy Island, Northumberland, TD15 2SJ.

Changing tides mean visitors to Northumberland's Holy Island are often against the clock to explore the square mile isle, though you'd never tell with the haul of caffeine hungry tourists taking time over a good brew at Pilgrims Coffee House.

Owner Andrew Mundy roasts the Holy Grail house blend and a selection of single origins in a converted yurt out back, meaning the coffee is as fresh as the hearty homemade fodder filling the menu. Soups, sarnies and gluttonous goodies are often organic, made with ingredients from the local indies and form the perfect fuel for onward expeditions.

INSIDER'S TIP
PILGRIMS' SCONES ARE LEGENDARY. THE ONLY QUESTION IS: PLAIN OR FRUIT?

If you can afford an hour or two to savour a few filters, there's plenty of seating at the historic farmhouse. Sink into one of the sofas in front of a roaring fire in winter or fight for a table in the spacious garden in summer.

Sustainability is key at this family friendly cafe; take-out cups are compostable, as are the bags in which you'll haul your bounty of beans home.

KEY ROASTER
Pilgrims Coffee

BREWING METHODS
Espresso,
batch brew

MACHINE
Fiorenzato San
Marco 3 group

GRINDERS
Anfim Super
Caimano,
Mahlkonig Peak

OPENING HOURS
Mon-Sun
9.30am-5pm
Dependent on tides

 Gluten FREE

 COFFEE BEANS AVAILABLE

 ALTERNATIVE MILK

 WIFI

 CYCLE FRIENDLY

 OUTDOOR seating

 FAMILY FRIENDLY

 DISABLED ACCESS

 BRING YOUR OWN Cup

---

www.pilgrimscoffee.com T: 01289 389109

f Pilgrims Coffee 🐦 @pilgrimscoffee 📷 @pilgrimscoffee

MORE GOOD
CUPS

So many cool places to drink coffee ...

MAP 58
WINDRUSH CAFE
Struan, Isle of Skye, IV56 8FB.

www.morbooks.co.uk

MAP 59
CAFE SIA
Broadford, Isle of Skye, IV49 9AB.

www.cafesia.co.uk

MAP 60
TAPA ORGANIC - KILMACOLM
12 St James Terrace,
Lochwinnoch Road, PA13 4HB.

www.tapacoffee.com

MAP 61
MEADOW ROAD
579 Dunbarton Road, Glasgow, G11 6HY.

MAP 62
SIEMPRE
162 Dumbarton Road, Glasgow, G11 6XE.

www.siemprebicyclecafe.com

MAP 63
PENA
5 Eton Lane, Glasgow, G12 8NB.

MAP 64
KELVIN POCKET
72 South Woodside Road,
Glasgow, G4 9HG.

www.kelvinpocket.co.uk

MAP 65
THE STEAMIE
1024 Argyle Street, Glasgow, G3 8LX.

www.thesteamie.co.uk

MAP 66
COFFEE CHOCOLATE AND TEA
944 Argyle Street, Glasgow, G3 8YJ.

MAP 67
LABORATORIO ESPRESSO
93 West Nile Street, Glasgow, G1 2SH.

www.laboratorioespresso.com

68
RIVERHILL COFFEE BAR
24 Gordon Street, Glasgow, G1 3PU.

www.riverhillcafe.com

69
PAPERCUP COFFEE COMPANY - CITY CENTRE
Located inside FORTY clothing,
11 Royal Exchange Square,
Glasgow, G1 3AJ.

www.papercupcoffee.co.uk

70
ALL THAT IS COFFEE
60 Osborne Street, Glasgow, G1 5QH.

71
STAN'S STUDIO
43 Alexandra Park Street,
Glasgow, G31 2UB.

www.stans-studio.com

72
TAPA ORGANIC - DENNISTOUN
19-21 Whitehill Street,
Glasgow, G31 2LH.

www.tapacoffee.com

73
BACK TO BLACK
bakery47, 76 Victoria Road,
Glasgow, G42 7AA.

www.backtoblackcoffee.co.uk

74
COFFEE ON WOOER
2-4 Wooer Street, Falkirk, FK1 1NJ.

www.coffeeonwooer.co.uk

75
GAMMA TRANSPORT DIVISION
6 Dean Park Street, Stockbridge,
Edinburgh, EH4 1JW.

www.gammatransportdivision.com

MAP.Nº 76
ARTISAN ROAST - STOCKBRIDGE
100a Raeburn Place,
Edinburgh, EH4 1HH.

www.artisanroast.co.uk

MAP.Nº 77
SÖDERBERG CAFE
- STOCKBRIDGE
3 Deanhaugh Street, Edinburgh, EH4 1LU.

www.soderberg.uk

MAP.Nº 78
GROUNDS OF STOCKBRIDGE
22 Deanhaugh Street,
Edinburgh, EH4 1LY.

www.groundsofstockbridge.com

MAP.Nº 79
TWELVE TRIANGLES
90 Brunswick Street,
Edinburgh, EH7 5HU.

www.twelvetriangles.com

MAP.Nº 80
PEP & FODDER
11 Waterloo Place,
Edinburgh, EH1 3BG.

www.pepandfodder.com

MAP.Nº 81
DOVECOT CAFE BY LEO'S
Dovecot Studios, 10 Infirmary Street,
Edinburgh, EH1 1LT.

www.dovecotstudios.com/gallery/cafe

MAP.Nº 82
SÖDERBERG CAFE
- QUARTERMILE
27 Simpson Loan, Edinburgh, EH3 9GG.

www.soderberg.uk

MAP.Nº 83
SÖDERBERG BAKERY SHOP
- QUARTERMILE
33 Simpson Loan, Edinburgh, EH3 9GG

www.soderberg.uk

Nº84
THE COUNTER – TOLLCROSS
Police Box, High Riggs, Tollcross,
Edinburgh, EH3 9RP.

Nº85
PEKOETEA
20 Leven Street, Edinburgh, EH3 9LJ.

www.pekoetea.co.uk

Nº86
ARTISAN ROAST – BRUNTSFIELD
138 Bruntsfield Place,
Edinburgh, EH10 4ER.

www.artisanroast.co.uk

Nº87
SALT CAFE
56 Morningside Road,
Edinburgh, EH10 4BZ.

Nº88
THE COUNTER – MORNINGSIDE
Police Box, 216a Morningside Road,
Edinburgh, EH10 4QQ.

Nº89
SÖDERBERG BAKERY SHOP – WEST END
31 Queensferry Street,
Edinburgh, EH2 4QS.

www.soderberg.uk

Nº90
CHAPTER ONE COFFEE SHOP
107-109 Dalry Road,
Edinburgh, EH11 2DR.

www.chapterone.coffee

Nº91
THE LITTLE GREEN VAN
Portobello Promenade,
Edinburgh, EH15 2BS.

ROASTERS

^{MAP№}92. MACBEANS

2 Little Belmont Street, Aberdeen, AB10 1JG.
www.macbeans.com T: 01224 624757

f MacBeans Coffee & Tea 🐦 @macbeanscoffee ⊡ @macbeans

Speciality coffee may be the choice drink of the contemporary hipster crowd but when Ian Cukrowski first opened award winning MacBeans in 1989 in Aberdeen, that was hardly the case.

And while the original clientele might have been older coffee lovers, today a wide demographic seek out this charming shop and roastery, which, using reclaimed wood, was set up to look like an old-school apothecary.

'Coffee has become like wine and people are a lot more knowledgeable,' says Ian. *'So we like to cater for everyone's tastes.'*

The shop still exudes a traditional old-world vibe. Iconic royal blue containers line the walls, housing a host of light and dark in-house roasts. While staff enjoy going the extra mile for mail order customers by adding hand drawn pictures to every package.

'It was started by one of the girls working here who was also an artist,' laughs Ian, who's keen to maintain this personal touch to the popular mail order service.

'She began drawing on the packets and it's become a unique feature of the business. It got such great feedback from our customers that they now expect it.'

Ian, a former offshore chemist, began looking for a radical life change after being left badly shaken when close colleagues were killed in the 1988 Piper Alpha explosion.

The idea for the coffee shop hit him after visiting tea and coffee merchant, Braithwaite in Dundee. *'I thought "why can't I bring this quality of tea and coffee to Aberdeen?".'* The rest, as they say, is history.

'COFFEE HAS BECOME LIKE WINE AND PEOPLE ARE A LOT MORE KNOWLEDGEABLE'

And when he's not in the basement, roasting one of the 20 single origins or 10 bespoke blends, Ian's globe-trotting to Kenya, Guatemala, Brazil and other growing destinations, keeping Aberdonians and those further afield supplied with superb quality coffee.

≡93. SACRED GROUNDS COFFEE COMPANY

Unit 15, Arbroath Business Centre, 31 Dens Road, Arbroath, Angus, DD11 1RS.

www.sacredgroundscoffeecompany.co.uk   T: 07808 806610

f Sacred Grounds Coffee Company   🐦 @sacredgrounds14   📷 @sacred_grounds_coffee_company

Based on the banks of the Brothock Burn in Arbroath, Sacred Grounds Coffee Company is Angus's first and only speciality roastery.

And having only started roasting in December 2015, owners Kathryn, Jamie and Ian are out to build a reputation for outstanding quality.

'We want to educate, inspire and enthuse the people of Angus and beyond,' says coffee lover Kathryn who, after 20 years in hospitality, was invited to run the roasting business alongside her bean-nut brother Ian and pro roaster, Jamie.

The other valued member of the team is Fatima – their 5kg Toper roaster. She's enjoyed a long history in the Scottish roasting community and is still producing cracking coffee in her new home.

'She may not be the most high-tech, glamorous piece of kit but she's a really excellent worker,' laughs Kathryn.

The team buys premium green beans from ethical and sustainable sources before cooking them up. *'Everything takes time. We don't rush our roasting – but it's worth it,'* says Kathryn. *'Our reason for existing is simple – to produce the most fabulous coffee.'*

'GRIND IT JUST BEFORE YOU BREW AND RESPECT THE 400-PLUS MAN HOURS THAT HAVE GONE INTO PRODUCING A SINGLE CUP'

Single origin coffee beans are sold online – with the key word being 'beans'.

'Our coffee is sacred once ground,' explains Kathryn. *'So to ensure quality, we encourage people to grind their beans at home.'*

She's not being esoteric – the reason for the advice is that coffee deteriorates quickly once ground.

'Grind it just before you brew and respect the 400-plus man hours that have gone into producing a single cup of coffee,' she suggests. *'You won't regret it.'*

№94. GLEN LYON COFFEE ROASTERS

COFFEE COURSES AVAILABLE | COFFEE BEANS AVAILABLE | ONLINE | ONSITE

Aberfeldy Business Park, Dunkeld Road, Aberfeldy, Perthshire, PH15 2AQ.

www.glenlyoncoffee.co.uk   T: 01887 822817

f Glen Lyon Coffee   🐦 @glenlyoncoffee   © @glenlyoncoffee

It's been six years since Fiona Grant started roasting coffee at her bothy in Glen Lyon, one of the most stunning spots in the Scottish Highlands.

Since those early days the roastery has expanded to Aberfeldy, where a talented team of five cook up beans on the 12kg Probat, cup coffees in the lab and pull heavenly espressos through the much-loved La Marzocco Linea.

Fiona first caught the coffee bug in Bolivia where she was working as a journalist. It's also where she met her husband and future business partner Jamie, so beans from the South American country are particularly close to their hearts.

'We always love to have a Bolivian coffee come through our roastery doors,' says Fiona, who buys beans seasonally so that a variety of coffees are offered throughout the year.

'We're also always excited about new season Rwandan and Ugandan coffees and often have a really good quality organic coffee in stock.'

Traceability and social responsibility are important to the couple, who love the fact that they can tell you the name of the farmer who grew your coffee as well as being able to divulge the stories behind the beans.

'We like to travel to origin as much as possible to build long-lasting, close relationships with our farmers,' says Fiona, who has a visit to Antioquia in Colombia in the pipeline.

'WE LIKE TO TRAVEL TO ORIGIN AS MUCH AS POSSIBLE TO BUILD LONG-LASTING RELATIONSHIPS'

When not roasting coffee, Jamie and Fiona are more often than not out exploring the Highlands.

'We love our Highland home and count ourselves incredibly lucky to have so many outdoor adventures on our doorstep.

'And of course, we're proud to supply so many fantastic businesses with our speciality beans.'

MAP№ 95. THE BEAN SHOP

67 George Street, Perth, PH1 5LB.
www.thebeanshop.co.uk   T: 01738 449955

f The Bean Shop   🐦 @thebeanshopuk   📷 @thebeanshopuk

With early insights into the speciality industry, it was no wonder that John and Lorna Bruce would start roasting coffee together when they met in Aberdeen.

Growing up on a tea plantation in Darjeeling, John developed a keen palate and passion for the bean, while Lorna's part-time student job at one of Scotland's first indie coffee roasters kick started her 19 years' of roasting experience.

Over a decade after launching The Bean Shop in a quiet corner of Perth's city centre, the duo still supply the busy little shop with beans roasted on the original 5kg Probat burrowed in the basement. And to keep up with increasing demand, new Loring and Sivet roasters have been introduced to take care of the house blend for the clan of wholesale customers.

'A STRICT ROAST-TO-ORDER RULE RESULTS IN A LIP-SMACKINGLY FRESH YIELD'

A sweeping selection of exotic coffees from around the world means the pioneering Probat is still doing its nine to five, with a strict roast-to-order rule on wholesale orders resulting in a lip-smackingly fresh yield.

Specialist coffees such as Colombian Geisha and Ethiopian Yirgacheffe often make an appearance on the shop's extensive menu, alongside beans from its direct relationship with farms in Honduras and Peru.

Shelves stacked with the latest brewing gear, slick ceramics and speciality teas make the shop a must-visit for the home enthusiast – visitors even get a wee taste of the latest espresso. Although its website and subscription service are on hand if you can't make it to Perth for your morning pick-me-up.

THOMSON'S COFFEE ROASTERS

№ 101

₌₉₆. HOME GROUND COFFEE

Lyleston West Lodge, Cardross, Dumbarton, Argyll and Bute, G82 5HF.

www.homegroundcoffee.co.uk   T: 01389 841730

f Home Ground Coffee 🐦 @the_coffee_guy © @homegroundcoffee

A quest to convert the hospitality industry to the thrills of speciality coffee is an all-consuming passion for Alastair Moodie, who started his bean business eight years ago in an old telephone exchange.

From those humble beginnings, Home Ground, which creates bespoke blends for cafes, restaurants and hotels, has gone on to clock up a clutch of prestigious gigs, including being the first to serve cold brew (way before it became a trend) at Latitude Festival, and supplying coffee to the Commonwealth Games.

This past year has been equally trailblazing, with a pop-up coffee shop in a forest with the Hinterland Project and the opening of a coffee shop at Calmac Ferry Terminal with foodie cooperative Food From Argyll.

'We've also started working with Milk Cafe in Glasgow – a social enterprise that helps female asylum seekers and immigrants – by designing a blend especially for the cause, which includes a Peruvian coffee called Femino.'

It's this willingness to design bespoke coffee for customers and train them in how to brew and serve it which characterises the family-run roastery.

'It's all about our customers and, of course, making sure all the coffee we roast and sell is of a very high quality and ethical standard,' says Alastair.

Nowadays he roasts his carefully selected beans from across the world on a 5kg Probat. *'We help customers to get the best out of our coffee and we have a passion for sharing our knowledge.'*

'HOME GROUND WAS THE FIRST TO SERVE COLD BREW (WAY BEFORE IT BECAME A TREND) AT LATITUDE FESTIVAL'

Single origin coffees and carefully balanced blends in natural compostable bags, freshly roasted to order by Alastair can be ordered through the website.

MAP №. 97. ROUNDSQUARE ROASTERY

Unit 4, Lorne Arcade, 115 High Street, Ayr, KA7 1QL.
www.roundsquareroastery.co.uk   T: 08009 992101

f Roundsquare Roastery   🐦 @roundsquareayr   📷 @roundsquarecoffeeroastery

It was the lack of traceable, sustainable and phenomenal speciality coffee in Ayrshire that motivated Lucas Berraud, Heather Stevenson and Partenie McGuigan to set up their own roastery.

After buying a small Probat test roaster, the trio began a long journey of trial and error, until they were satisfied that every bean leaving their premises had a beautifully balanced taste profile.

'We wanted to create a successful and ethically-sound business and a quality product that we could establish and grow over the coming years,' says Lucas.

'OAK CHIPPINGS SOAKED IN ARRAN SINGLE MALT GIVES OUR WHISKY CASK COFFEE A UNIQUE FLAVOUR'

And grow it they did. Upgrading the roasting gear to a Toper 10 and adding sales virtuoso Andrew O'Donnell to the crew, the small and passionate team aren't just dedicated to the art of creating great coffee, but to the whole process – from farm to cup.

Whether that's using direct trade with family-run farms in South and Central America; opening a stylish speciality coffee house in Edinburgh's Morningside; or providing machinery, grinders and specialist equipment and barista training for its customers.

And, of course, there's the coffee itself. The fruity House Blend, with its caramel undertones, is a Great Taste award winner, while the unique Whisky Cask Coffee sees the House Blend infused with Arran whisky before being cold smoked in a distillery cask.

'We built a smoker and have been perfecting this coffee with various types of wood chippings until hitting on the perfect recipe – oak chippings soaked in Arran single malt – for a unique flavour.'

ᴹᴬᴾ Nº 98. AVENUE COFFEE ROASTING CO.

COFFEE COURSES AVAILABLE | COFFEE BEANS AVAILABLE | ONLINE | ONSITE

321 Great Western Road, Glasgow, G4 9HR.

www.avenue.coffee   T: 01413 870249

f Avenue Coffee   🐦 @avenue_coffee   📷 @avenuecoffeeglasgow

'We're feeling a bit braver with what we do with the coffee this year,' says Todd Whiteford of Avenue. And crikey, it shows.

Where this time last year the team was buying greens from a single importer, they've now expanded the range to include exciting coffees from Cafe Imports, Nordic Approach and Falcon Speciality.

'BARISTA RYAN IS COMPETING IN THE WORLD COFFEE IN GOOD SPIRITS COMPETITION'

It's all part of the exciting journey that this roaster, with its two cafes in the city on Great Western Road (below the roastery) and Byres Road, is currently undertaking. Todd says that one of the reasons for the accelerated growth is the addition of roaster Courtney to the team. 'Courtney's experience has taken us up a level in terms of quality and efficiency,' says Todd, 'so we're doing 50 per cent more than a year ago.'

Roasting speciality grade coffee, and crafting a range of single origin filters and espresso blends that are hand roasted in small batches, means that they can be obsessive about quality. And that's brought them to the attention of the Fallen Brewing Company in Stirlingshire, with which Avenue has collaborated to create a coffee oatmeal pale ale known as The Steamer. It's aromatic and unusually easy drinking.

Other adventures for Avenue this year include the launch of coffee cocktails at its cafes (barista Ryan is competing in the World Coffee in Good Spirits competition) as well as hosting the Scottish premier of The Coffee Man at The Lighthouse in Glasgow.

Customers can drink the full range at the two Avenue cafes, (as well as across the city), and buy the beans and equipment to take home. We'll raise a glass to that.

[№]99. DEAR GREEN COFFEE ROASTERS

COFFEE BEANS AVAILABLE — ONLINE · ONSITE

COFFEE COURSES AVAILABLE

Unit 2, 13-27 East Campbell Street, Glasgow, G1 5DT.

www.deargreencoffee.com   T: 01415 527774

f Dear Green Coffee Roasters 🐦 @CoffeeGlasgow 📷 @deargreen

Masterminding many of the events that kick started Glasgow's thriving coffee culture, Dear Green's Lisa Lawson plays a significant role in supporting the city's speciality scene.

If launching the Glasgow Coffee Festival, Scottish AeroPress Championship, Roasting Championship and working with the EU Roasters Guild wasn't enough, Lisa is also the brains behind Scotland's first 100 per cent speciality roaster.

'We've always been committed to quality and our buying decisions have continued to endorse ethical trade throughout the chain,' she says.

Supplying speciality shops from Brighton to Orkney since 2011, Dear Green sources green beans from around the world from both importers and direct trade relationships. *'I've already got plans to visit Kenya and Colombia in 2017,'* says Lisa. *'After our big roastery move at the end of 2015 I've got a whole year of origin trips to catch up on.'*

The team's transition into a spacious new venue has also allowed Dear Green to expand its teaching potential, and with Lisa

qualifying as a SCA authorised trainer in 2016, it's the only roastery in Scotland where you can take approved sensory and barista courses.

'DEAR GREEN IS THE ONLY ROASTERY IN SCOTLAND WHERE YOU CAN TAKE APPROVED SENSORY AND BARISTA COURSES'

The busy roastery has decided to focus on the quality and constant innovation of its coffee this year.

'Our buying decisions are very focused now,' explains Lisa. *'We used to impulse buy but that would often mean that we could only roast a crop a couple of times and it was gone. This way we can make sure the quality of the roast is exceptional and keep providing our customers with the best coffee possible.'*

Along with its dedication to sourcing and roasting the very best speciality coffee, the passionate team – including current Scottish AeroPress Champion and top ranking roaster James Aitken – will this year be passing on its combined experience via the internationally recognised Coffee Diploma System.

MAP № 100. DEAR GREEN COFFEE ROASTERS

COFFEE BEANS AVAILABLE / ONLINE / ONSITE

COFFEE COURSES AVAILABLE

Unit 2, 13-27 East Campbell Street, Glasgow, G1 5DT.
www.deargreencoffee.com   T: 01415 527774

f Dear Green Coffee Roasters   🐦 @CoffeeGlasgow   📷 @deargreen

Offering free training to its loyal clan of customers since the roaster roared into action in 2011, Glasgow's Dear Green Coffee has kick started the coffee careers of some of the city's finest baristas.

Moving into a spacious new roastery last year, owner Lisa Lawson and her talented team have finally been able to expand their teaching potential.

'It's something we've always done but never had the space to shout about it,' says Lisa. *'We've always invited our wholesale customers to come in and learn the basics with us because when a coffee has our name on it, we want it to be served the best it can be.'*

'TAILORED BARISTA TRAINING COVERS EVERYTHING FROM ESPRESSO EXTRACTION TO MILK TEXTURISING'

Passing her AST qualifications in 2016, Lisa is now one of a handful of SCA authorised trainers in the UK, making Dear Green the only roastery in Scotland where you can take SCA approved sensory and barista courses. *'These are tailored to baristas who want to hone in on the scientific and sensory elements of espresso,'* explains Lisa.

For novices and start-up shops, tailored barista training covers everything from espresso extraction to milk texturising, with both group and one-to-one sessions available. Students are in the experienced hands of seasoned barista trainer Darryl Docherty, a former Scottish Barista Champ and 2017 UKBC competitor.

Along with the internationally recognised Coffee Diploma qualifications, brew workshops cater to hobbyists who want to get the most out of their speciality beans at home.

As well as sharing her knowledge from the East Campbell Street venue, and sitting on the committee of the EU Roasters Guild, Lisa has been teaching coffee at colleges around Glasgow.

'Some students didn't even realise that coffee comes from cherries, so it's been great to introduce an insight into speciality for those going into the hospitality industry. It feels as if we're going full circle, which is really exciting.'

MAP № 101. THOMSON'S COFFEE ROASTERS

COFFEE BEANS AVAILABLE ONLINE □ ONSITE 🛒

Burnfield Avenue, Glasgow, G46 7TL.
www.thomsonscoffee.com   T: 01416 370683

f Thomsons Coffee   🐦 @thomsonscoffee   📷 @thomsonscoffee

The Thomson's story stretches back 175 years with many pioneering firsts – from David Thomson opening Scotland's first speciality coffee shop in 1841 to the manufacture of curious contraptions like the Napier Coffee Apparatus (a forerunner to the modern syphon).

'THOMSON'S REMAINS TRUE TO ITS HERITAGE, COMBINING TRADITIONAL ROASTING TECHNIQUES AND STATE-OF-THE-ART TECHNOLOGY'

Scotland's original coffee roaster is still an independently-owned family business with a rich heritage to draw upon.

Thomson's has embraced its history with traditional methods of the past alongside the latest available technology.

'Thomson's remains true to its heritage and pioneering spirit by combining traditional roasting techniques on antique flame roasters and Scotland's first state-of-the-art Loring Smart Roaster,' says managing director Russell Jenkins.

The result is an impressive range of high quality single origin and small batch coffees right through to favourites from the past and blends with real provenance.

Being in the coffee business for so many years has great advantages when it comes to importing the best quality beans, with more than 40 years of relationship building.

And Thomson's likes to work very closely with its coffee growers.

'In 2016 we sent some of our team to work on a farm with one of our trusted producers in Colón Genova in the north of Colombia's world-famous Nariño.

'These unique opportunities help us share information directly with the farmers and forge stronger, more meaningful relationships that will last well into the future,' says Russell.

In 2017, the dedicated team will bring Thomson's presence back to the centre of Glasgow where it all started 175 years ago. Watch this space ...

102. OVENBIRD COFFEE ROASTERS

COFFEE COURSES AVAILABLE | COFFEE BEANS AVAILABLE | ONLINE ONSITE

Block b, Unit 2, 45 Glenwood Place, Glasgow, G45 9UH.

www.ovenbird.co.uk   T: 01416 340309

f Ovenbird Coffee Roasters   🐦 @ovenbird_coffee   📷 @ovenbird_coffee

Davide Angeletti of Ovenbird may be Italian by birth, but with the creation of his new whisky barrel-aged coffee, he's about to be a one-man Scottish coffee ambassador, taking his Glasgow-roasted speciality beans to the world.

Such is the interest in this venture, which launched in November 2016 ('*after a year finding the right recipe and the right ingredients*'), that he's receiving orders from Japan and the US and is showcasing the coffee at a number of food festivals via Scotland Food and Drink.

'*The feedback has been overwhelming,*' says Davide. '*We are aging single origin, Malawian and Rwandan green beans for up to eight weeks in Scottish whisky barrels from distilleries AnCnoc and Auchentoshan.*

'*During the process we roll the barrels regularly to make sure that all of the green beans are exposed to the aroma from the wood and then roast them to a medium roast to complement the whisky flavour.*

'*There is nothing quite like it and the flavour profile is one of chocolate, sweet tobacco, cherry and whisky, resulting in a very aromatic, mildly bright and smooth cup with a velvety body and long finish.*'

Of course, this is not the only coffee that Davide and colleagues are working with. This year they're also exploring new African coffees, particularly one from the Congo, via bean importer, Schluter. '*It's my favourite new discovery,*' smiles Davide, '*and I'm very happy that as part of the project we are also helping to support farmers.*'

'WE ARE AGING SINGLE ORIGIN MALAWIAN AND RWANDAN GREEN BEANS IN WHISKY BARRELS FOR UP TO EIGHT WEEKS'

Ovenbird has also introduced a new Tanzanian peaberry and a new Ethiopian decaff. '*I'm not really into decaff,*' Davide confesses, '*but it's very important to provide a good one and I'm very pleased with this – I don't think you can even tell it's decaffeinated.*'

103. FORTITUDE COFFEE ROASTERS

Unit 6, New Broompark Business Park, Edinburgh, EH5 1RS.
www.fortitudecoffeeroasters.com

f Fortitude Coffee 🐦 @fortitudecoffee 📷 @fortitudecoffee

After three years' experience running Fortitude Coffee, a popular cafe on the Edinburgh speciality scene, Matt Carroll and business partner Helen Coburn are ready to embrace the next step in their coffee journey: roasting at their bespoke unit in the city.

'I gained a little experience in roasting and I just love the creative element,' says Matt, who is inspired by the lighter, sweeter roast styles of the Nordic coffee scene and companies such as Drop Coffee.

'IT'S GREAT TO FEEL AT ONE WITH YOUR MACHINE AND GET IT TO WORK AS YOU WANT'

'Since then I've been working away and learning new techniques.

'It's fascinating to discover the clear differences that occur in the cup when you change something in the roast. I can get quite obsessed.

'And it's great to feel at one with your machine and to get it to work as you want.'

Matt and Helen focus on small batches of single origin coffee at their micro roastery by the Firth.

'When roasting, we look to develop coffee with a singular character and a clean, sweet taste,' says Matt, who uses a 12kg Diedrich roaster and enjoys combining creativity with exacting quality controls.

'We work with a small number of high quality green bean suppliers when sourcing our coffee and are proud to provide complete traceability from farm to cup.'

Fortitude offers training to wholesale customers, an online shop and regular cuppings.

'We believe good quality coffee is a simple pleasure to enjoy every day,' says Matt.

The new venture is proving a heady experience for Matt and Helen, who are looking forward to even more caffeine collaborations with like-minded people in 2017.

OVENBIRD COFFEE ROASTERS
№ 102

104. WILLIAMS AND JOHNSON COFFEE CO.

Customs Wharf, Edinburgh, EH6 6PL (cafe address).
www.williamsandjohnson.com T: 07542 974642

f Williams and Johnson Coffee Co.   🐦 @wjcoffee   📷 @williamsandjohnson

Tucked away in a former biscuit factory in Leith, Todd Johnson and Zachary Williams are focused less on bourbon biscuits and more on bourbon coffee beans as they build their burgeoning speciality roasting business.

Todd earned his chops at Market Lane Coffee in Melbourne, while Zachary worked at Steampunk Coffee in North Berwick. However, it was as a result of meeting while they were both employed at Artisan Roast in Edinburgh that they decided to break away [enough biscuit puns already – Ed] and go it alone.

'WE'RE DRIVEN BY OUR FAVOURITE BEANS AND CUPPING ALL THE BLOODY TIME'

Williams and Johnson started roasting in January 2016 and by their own admission have been taking their time, but hey, that's the way the cookie crumbles.

'We wanted to develop our roasting style, to be sure that we got it spot on before we went to market,' says Todd.

That style turns out to be a dedication to 'bright, juicy, premium coffees'.

Zachary says, 'our cupping table is a shrine to high altitude, high grade coffees. We're driven by our favourite beans and cupping all the bloody time.

'Our passion is in sharing beautiful coffees. We think coffee is a very special treat and that every cup should be worth it.

'It's a pleasure for us to taste heaps of new harvest coffees from around the globe and build our offering out of only exceptional beans, produced by people who really care.'

Caffeine fiends can taste the pair's latest roasts as espresso or filter at the flagship cafe on Edinburgh's Custom Lane, where a drool-worthy line-up of doughnuts, bakes and locally sourced sarnies keep the coffee offering company. The city's Cairngorm and Filament Coffee also stock the boys' beans – just don't ask if you can dunk your biscuit in.

℥105. COFFEE NEXUS

8 Howard Street, Edinburgh, EH3 5JP.
coffeenexus.co.uk   T: 01315 561430

f Coffee Nexus Ltd   🐦 @coffeenexus   📷 @coffeenexus

When it comes to blazing the bean trail, Coffee Nexus' John Thompson is a firebrand who deals in firsts.

His training and consultancy lab held the first Coffee Quality Institute Q Robusta course recently, making John both a rare qualified Q grader, but also Scotland's first R grader (one of only three in the UK). He's also had a key role in the curriculum development of the Speciality Coffee Association's (SCA) Coffee Diploma System, helping create content for the green coffee, roasting and sensory modules.

Add to that his position as head judge at the International Cup of Excellence (an award scheme run across 10 countries, helping farmers access high quality roasters) and it's plain to see why he's the go-to man for roasteries and coffee brands of all sizes, which are seeking advice and training.

As well as certifying more than 100 people in SCA cupping, roasting and green coffee at his Edinburgh lab in the last year, John has been helping customers improve and develop their roasting, sourcing and products.

'At the heart of our success in developing new products for businesses is knowing that every project has to be dealt with in a unique way,' he says.

A passion for quality, diversity of coffee and the people behind the bean are key drivers for John, whose career in speciality coffee started in the 1990s with projects ranging from field, through to roasting and retail.

'Coffee Nexus works to add value and increase sustainability in the supply chain. We do this through consultancy, training and product testing, starting in the coffee fields and running all the way through to finished projects for coffee drinkers.'

'WE KNOW EVERY PRODUCT HAS TO BE DEALT WITH IN A UNIQUE WAY'

All that, and there's still time for encouraging a bit of healthy competition. For the past two years Coffee Nexus has co-hosted the UK Roasters Championship, alongside Dear Green Coffee Roasters.

≞106. MR EION COFFEE ROASTER

COFFEE COURSES AVAILABLE | COFFEE BEANS AVAILABLE | ONSITE

9 Dean Park Street, Stockbridge, Edinburgh, EH4 1JN.

www.mreion.com   T: 01313 431354

f Mr. Eion: Coffee Roaster   🐦 @mr_eion   📷 @mr_eion

The grown up equivalent of a sweetie shop, Eion Henderson's (that's Mr Eion to you) roastery-come-bean-store in Edinburgh's Stockbridge area is bursting with such a wide variety of freshly roasted beans that it's more appealing than any pick 'n' mix.

And while roasting is going on right in the shop on Big Blue, the 5kg Diedrich roaster, customers are almost constantly popping in for a coffee bean top up and a bit of chat with Eion and his colleagues Meave, Scott and Cameron.

'WE'RE LOOKING FORWARD TO SHOWCASING SOME NEW COFFEES FROM HONDURAS IN 2017'

Piled-high bags of greens, courtesy of importer DRWakefield, add authenticity to the scene while an impressive selection of kit, including must-have Harris Tweed covered cafetieres and colourful enamel coffee pots all provide a cheerful vibe in this friendly neighbourhood store.

Sourcing unusual beans and microlots that are not widely available, the team is part of Project 121, *'which provides benefits of direct trade, such as sustainability, traceability, quality and social justice for small scale roasters like ourselves,'* says Eion.

'It's given us access to the beautiful chocolate, hazelnut and cherry qualities of the Peruvian Pan De Arbol beans, and we're looking forward to showcasing some new coffees from Honduras in 2017.'

6-8 South College Street, Edinburgh, EH8 9AA.
www.brewlabcoffee.co.uk/training   T: 01316 628963

f Brew Lab Coffee   🐦 @brewlabcoffee   📷 @brewlabcoffee

ucked away under the floorboards of one of Edinburgh's leading coffee houses, Brew Lab Training Lab is steeping the next batch of badass baristas and coffee pulling pros in coffee knowledge.

Serving speciality up top and coaching a league of lever lovers below, the South College Street venue is a mecca for novices wanting to learn the trade.

Kitted out with all the latest gear, the underground lair may appear to be a playground for the professionals, but owners David Law and Tom Hyde have specifically created courses to cater to coffee capability of every level.

'BREW LAB'S TEAM TAUGHT THE EDINBURGH RUGBY TEAM HOW TO MAKE A RUDDY GOOD BREW'

Masterclasses range from the basics – learning to pull a shot, perfecting shop-standard latte art and brewing filter for the home – for the complete novice to bespoke sessions for the seasoned barista wanting to hone in on a particular skill.

Sensory classes are a new addition this year, designed to give an insight into speciality coffee and explore the diversity of available flavours.

With both an espresso and brew bar on hand, the training space is available to hire for those looking to sharpen a routine before a competition or who just want to brush up on basic skills away from the bustling shop floor.

Brew Lab's team also offer off-site training, and in 2016 even taught the Edinburgh Rugby team how to make a ruddy good brew.

108. ARTISAN ROAST COFFEE ROASTERS

COFFEE COURSES AVAILABLE | COFFEE BEANS AVAILABLE | ONLINE | ONSITE

Peffermill Industrial Estate, Kings Haugh, Unit 4, Edinburgh, EH16 5UY.

www.artisanroast.co.uk   T: 07590 590667

f Artisan Roast   🐦 @artisanroast   📷 @artisanroastcoffeeroasters

Artisan Roast's entrepreneurs Gustavo Pardo (the Chilean with a head for business) and Michael Wilson (the Kiwi who knows his beans) can be hailed as two of the great founding fathers of speciality coffee in Scotland.

Since setting up Scotland's first speciality roastery and cafe in 2007, accolades have been rolling in for their contribution to the scene, with numerous awards and praise in national newspapers and magazines. The team was completed in 2012 when John Thompson, one of Europe's leading coffee experts, joined as head roaster and sourcing expert.

At the leading edge of the new wave of the speciality coffee revolution, this team has built the Artisan brand on a potent trinity: great taste, ethical sourcing and contemporary, creative design.

Part of the secret, according to John, is in the sourcing:*'We source unique micro lots. Relationships are long term, built on travel and communication with quality focused producers. We're always adding new innovative coffees to our offerings, and also know our customers have firm favourites they love to see year in, year out.'*

Then there's the roast profiling and cafe lab, equipped with its 1kg Probatino. Artisan makes a point of never working with cupping notes created by someone else.

'FRESH COFFEE WHICH HAS DIVERSITY IN FLAVOUR PROFILE, POST-HARVEST PROCESS AND COFFEE CULTIVAR'

'We strive for absolute consistency in roasting so when people buy our coffee it tastes perfect every time. We have a custom built one-of-a-kind Diedrich for roasting micro lots and our team of award winning baristas at our four cafes provide relentless feedback on every roast. Before our coffee hits the shelves, the baristas and roasters have cupped it to make sure the taste is perfect.

'The aim is to offer our customers fresh coffee which has diversity in flavour profile, post-harvest process and coffee cultivar.'

This, along with innovative packaging, designed to aid customer choice, ensures the popularity of this innovative brand continues, not only with cafes across Scotland but also with its global fan base of online buyers.

№109. STEAMPUNK COFFEE

COFFEE BEANS AVAILABLE **ONLINE** **ONSITE**

49a Kirk Ports, North Berwick, East Lothian, EH39 4HL.
www.steampunkcoffee.co.uk   T: 01620 893030 (cafe no.)

f Steampunk Coffee 🐦 @steampunkcoffee 📷 @steampunkcoffee

Steampunk Coffee's humble roots began in 2012 when a lever espresso machine was installed in the back of Mavis, owner Cath Franks' trusty yellow 1976 VW camper.

Cath and Mavis began making appearances at markets and festivals, selling coffee sourced from indie roasters. Inspired by her success, Cath decided to equip her garage with a vintage Probat roaster and started sourcing and roasting beans.

'WE REMAIN IN TOUCH WITH OUR ROOTS AS WE CONTINUE TO SERVE COFFEE FROM THE VAN'

Over the next four years, while remaining strongly independent, the business grew steadily, fuelled by a passionate and ethically driven team of coffee geeks and supported by 'some wonderful wholesale partners'.

'We remain in touch with our roots as we continue to serve coffee from the van every Sunday at Stockbridge Market in Edinburgh. We also still supply many of our original cafe partners,' says Cath.

Today, the Steampunk Coffee roastery is housed in an atmospheric old warehouse in the centre of North Berwick. From here, head roaster Dori Czedgledi and her team create small batch speciality single origin coffees.

Beans are roasted and cupped, before being sent to wholesale partners, online buyers and Steampunk Coffee's own bustling on-site cafe.

The roastery works with green coffee merchants Nordic Approach and Falcon Speciality and is committed to ethical trading.

Beans are sold at the roastery and online, alongside a host of fun Steampunk branded stuff including mugs, camping cups, tote bags, buffs, bandanas – and even plectrums.

ᴹᴬᴾ ᴺᵒ 110. LUCKIE BEANS

3 Love Lane, Berwick-upon-Tweed, Northumberland, TD15 1AR.
www.luckiebeans.co.uk   T: 07810 446537

f Luckie Beans Coffee Roasters 🐦 @luckiebeans 📷 @luckie_beans

The morning commute has got that bit more attractive for coffee heads since Luckie Beans set up stall at Glasgow Queen Street train station last summer.

The waft of an award winning Love Lane house blend or the latest Queen Street blend from the smart new coffee cart is enough to perk up even the most jaded city worker.

With less than two weeks' notice to source the cart – which included finding an espresso machine and knowledgeable baristas - it was a whirlwind experience for owner Jamie McLuckie.

'IT'S LOOKING FANTASTIC SITTING IN GLASGOW QUEEN STREET TRAIN STATION'

'In previous lives the cart had been in a London Tube Station, a hospital in Essex and a bus station in South Wales,' he says. 'Now – after a lot of TLC – it's looking fantastic sitting in Glasgow Queen Street train station.'

Those in transit can languish in their good luck by lingering at the La Marzocco Linea with a choice of Luckie Beans freshly roasted coffees.

And pleased customers can also buy a bag of beans to grind at home. The labels have recently been blinged up with a gold-foiled logo, making each bag of coffee goodness as beautiful as it tastes.

A range of single origin beans and blends are also available to buy online where you can opt for the rather convenient letterbox friendly packaging, which means no more waiting in for the postie.

Jamie roasts all the beans in Berwick-upon-Tweed's Love Lane at an 18th century roastery, just metres from the sea. Roasting is carried out in small batches with a precision and care of which they are proud.

'Our slogan is "roasted with passion on Love Lane",' he adds. 'And at every stage in the process we focus on quality.'

MAP No. 111. PILGRIMS COFFEE

COFFEE BEANS AVAILABLE / ONLINE / ONSITE

Falkland House, Margate, Holy Island, Northumberland, TD15 2SJ.

www.pilgrimscoffee.com   T: 01289 389109

f Pilgrims Coffee   🐦 @pilgrimscoffee   📷 @pilgrimscoffee

Roasting coffee in a yurt on a tidal island off the coast of Northumberland throws up a few challenges; the sweltering heat in summer and freezing conditions of winter being just the tip of the iceberg. But after two and a half years (and a big old learning curve), Holy Island's first coffee roastery is pumping out the good stuff.

Head roaster Andrew Mundy has owned Pilgrims Coffee – one of the three cafes on the island – for a decade, but it wasn't until three years ago that his interest in speciality sprouted. *I started drinking it and thought, "wow! I should be serving this". And that quickly escalated to roasting,'* he explains.

A couple of years and roaster upgrades later, Andrew almost had his unique blend down. All that was required was a masterclass or two with John Thompson of Nexus, and Holy Island's first speciality coffee was ready for the cafe and the wider market.

'We keep things really seasonal and only order small batches of standout beans, so our house blend Holy Grail is always super fresh, showcasing different flavours throughout the year,' enthuses Andrew. *'Our single origin selection is also constantly changing.'*

To keep up with demand from a cluster of local coffee shops and Pilgrims' own popular cafe, Andrew has just brought in Jonny, who he's training up on the 10kg Ozturk gas drum roaster.

'ROASTING COFFEE IN A YURT ON A TIDAL ISLAND THROWS UP A FEW CHALLENGES'

Available to order online, Pilgrims' ethical endeavour to source incredible, fairly traded beans, packaged in the best biodegradable bags with compostable labels makes courier coffee a little easier on the conscience.

MORE GOOD
ROASTERS

112
SKYE ROASTERY
Cafe Sia, Broadford,
Isle of Skye, IV49 9AB.

www.cafesia.co.uk

113
UNORTHODOX ROASTERS
129 High Street, Kinross, KY13 8AQ.

www.unorthodoxroasters.co.uk

114
PAPERCUP COFFEE COMPANY
603 Great Western Road,
Glasgow, G12 8HX.

www.papercupcoffee.co.uk

115
TAPA COFFEE
721 Pollockshaws Road, Strathbungo,
Glasgow, G41 2AA.

www.tapacoffee.com

116
CHARLIE MILLS COFFEE
Eaglesham, Glasgow, G76 0BB.

www.charliemillscoffee.com

117
NORTHERN EDGE COFFEE
Unit 5, Meantime Workshops,
North Greenwich Road, Spittal,
Berwick-upon-Tweed, TD15 1RG.

www.northernedgecoffee.co.uk

SACRED GROUNDS COFFEE COMPANY
№ 93

COFFEE GLOSSARY

ESPRESSO

BARISTA

The multi-skilled pro making your delicious coffee drinks.

CHANNELING

When a small hole or crack in the coffee bed of espresso forms, resulting in the water bypassing the majority of the ground coffee.

DISTRIBUTION

The action of distributing coffee evenly inside the espresso basket before tamping to encourage even extraction. This can be achieved through tapping, shaking or smoothing the coffee out with your fingers.

DOSE

The amount of ground coffee used when preparing a coffee.

GOD-SHOT

The name given to a shot of espresso when all the variables are in line and the coffee tastes at its optimum.

GRAVIMETRIC

The term for an espresso machine with the technology to control the yield, based on coffee dose.

OCD

Tool used for distributing coffee inside the espresso.

PRESSURE PROFILING

The act of controlling the amount of pressure applied to espresso throughout the extraction time, resulting in different espresso flavours and styles.

ROSETTA

The name given to the fern-like latte art pattern served on the top of a flat white or other milk drink.

TAMP

The action of compacting coffee into the espresso basket with a tamper in order to encourage even extraction.

YIELD

The volume of liquid produced when preparing an espresso or brewed coffee. A traditional espresso would yield twice that of the coffee dose. For example if you use 18g of coffee to brew an espresso, then you might yield 36g of liquid.

FILTER

AGITATE
Stirring the coffee throughout the brew cycle when preparing filter coffee to increase strength or encourage even extraction.

BATCH BREW
Filter coffee prepared on a large scale using a filter coffee machine.

BLOOM
The action of pouring water on freshly ground coffee to evenly coat each coffee particle. This encourages even extraction.

BREW
The general term given to filter coffee – as opposed to espresso.

CASCARA
The outer skin of the coffee cherry can be used to make an infusion served hot like a tea or cold, mixed with sparkling water.

COFFEE BLOSSOM
The flowers collected from the coffee bush are dried and can be used to make a tea-like infusion.

COLD BREW
Coffee brewed using cold water and left to extract over a longer period. Served cold, this coffee has high sweetness and low acidity.

CUPPING
The international method used to assess coffee. The beans are ground to a coarse consistency and steeped in a bowl of hot water for four minutes before the crust of grounds is scraped away from the surface. The coffee is left to cool and assessed via a big slurp from a cupping spoon.

EK 43
Popular grinder used for both espresso and filter.

BEANS

ARABICA

The species of coffee commonly associated with speciality coffee, arabica is a delicate species which grows at high altitudes. It has lower levels of caffeine and typically higher perceived acidity, sweetness and a cleaner body.

BLEND

A blend of coffee from different farms and origins, traditionally used for espresso.

HONEY PROCESS

This process sits in-between washed and natural. The seeds are removed from the cherry and then left to dry with the mucilage intact, resulting in a sweet coffee with some characteristics of washed and natural process coffee.

NATURAL PROCESS

Naturally processed coffee is picked from the coffee bush and left to rest for a period of time with the fruit of the coffee cherry intact. In some cases the cherry can be left like this for two weeks before being hulled off. This results in a fruity, full body.

NINETY PLUS

All coffee is graded before sale with points out of 100. Speciality coffee will have 80 or more points. A coffee with 90 or more points is referred to as 90+ and will usually be quite exclusive, very tasty and expensive!

ROBUSTA

A low grade species of coffee, robusta grows at lower altitudes. This species has a high caffeine content and displays more bitterness and earthy flavours.

SINGLE ORIGIN

The term usually used for coffee from one origin. Single estate is the term used for coffee from one farm. Can be used for espresso or filter.

WASHED

Washed coffee is picked from the coffee bush and the outer layers of the cherry are immediately removed from the seed (what you normally call the coffee bean) and put into fermentation tanks to remove the layer of sticky mucilage before being laid out to dry. This washing process removes some of the sugars and bitterness so the coffee should have a higher acidity and lighter body.

Hannah Davies

'A COFFEE WITH 90 OR MORE POINTS WILL USUALLY BE QUITE EXCLUSIVE, TASTY AND EXPENSIVE!'

MEET OUR COMMITTEE

The Scottish Independent Coffee Guide's committee is made up of a small band of coffee experts and enthusiasts which has worked with Salt Media and the coffee community to oversee this year's guide

JOHN THOMPSON

LISA LAWSON

DAVE LAW

NICK COOPER

JOHN THOMPSON

John owns Coffee Nexus, a coffee consultancy in Edinburgh. As well as working with numerous coffee roasters, brands and farmers to improve sustainability and add value, John develops educational content with the SCA and is a head judge for the globally recognised Cup of Excellence programme. With a wealth of coffee knowledge behind him, John also co-wrote a manual for the Coffee Board of Malawi.

LISA LAWSON

Lisa is a mover and shaker in the Scottish speciality coffee scene, and set up and runs Dear Green Coffee Roasters, the first roastery in Glasgow to exclusively roast speciality grade coffee. She also kick started the Glasgow Coffee Festival and the Scottish AeroPress Championship. Lisa sources beans from across the globe and turns them into beautiful coffee which she supplies to cafes and direct to home baristas. In 2016, Lisa qualified as an authorised SCA trainer in sensory and barista skills and joined the committee of the EU Roasters Guild.

DAVE LAW

Co-owner of Brew Lab, Dave Law hasn't always been a coffee connoisseur. Fresh out of uni he spent four years researching and developing the Brew Lab concept with co-founder Tom Hyde before opening the coffee bar and barista training ground in Edinburgh. He's been immersed in the industry ever since. When he's not working at the lab, you'll find Dave on his bike, playing music and visiting coffee shops around the world with his wife.

NICK COOPER

Nick is one of the founding directors at Salt Media, a boutique publishing, design and marketing company that crafts the *Indy Coffee Guides*. His obsession with coffee started 15 years ago when he was living and working in Sydney. A couple of barista courses and a lot of flat whites later, he and wife Jo returned to the UK with a serious plan to open an Aussie style coffee shop. They ended up creating Salt Media instead, so now he gets his coffee kicks through his work on the guides.

COFFEE NOTES

Somewhere to save details of specific brews and beans you've enjoyed

COFFEE
NOTES

COFFEE
NOTES

COFFEE
NOTES